A Liminal Life

Antoinette "Tiyi" Schippers

A Liminal Life

A Medium's Memoir

BOOK 2 OF THE GATEKEEPER SERIES

Parkhurst Brothers Publishers

MARION, MICHIGAN

www.parkhurstbrothers.com

Consumers may order Parkhurst Brothers books from their favorite online or bricks-and-mortar booksellers, expecting prompt delivery. Parkhurst Brothers books are distributed to the trade through the Chicago Distribution Center. Trade and library orders may be placed through Ingram Book Company, Baker & Taylor, Follett Library Resources and other book industry wholesalers. To order from Chicago Distribution Center, phone 1-800-621-2736 or fax to 800-621-8476. Copies of this and other Parkhurst Brothers Publishers titles are available to organizations and corporations for purchase in quantity by contacting Special Sales Department at our home office location, listed on our web site. Manuscript submission guidelines for this publishing company are available at our web site.

Printed in the United States of America
First Edition, April, 2023
Printing history: 2025 2024 2023   8 7 6 5 4 3 2 1
Library Cataloging Data

1. Author–Schippers, Antoinette "Tiyi", American storyteller and author
2. Subject–Paranormal, Americana
3. Subject–Spirits, Mediums

2023-trade paperback and e-book

ISBN: Trade Paperback   978-1-62491-196-5
ISBN: e-book   978-1-62491-197-2

Parkhurst Brothers Publishers believes that the free and open exchange of ideas is essential for the maintenance of our freedoms. We support the First Amendment of the United States Constitution and encourage all citizens to study all sides of public policy questions, making up their own minds.

Interior design by   Linda D. Parkhurst PhD
Acquired for Parkhurst Brothers Publishers by   Ted Parkhurst
Cover art by   Rachael Davis
042023

DEDICATION

I dedicate this book to the many angels, allies, and adversaries whom I encountered along my path. Those who enlightened or enhanced my journey, as well as those who challenged me, forging my spirit stronger, with an ability to witness wondrous things unseen.

ACKNOWLEDGMENTS

Many thanks to my family and friends who encourage me to tell my story. To my children Rachael, Zak, Arra, and Ezra who accept and honor my gifts freely. Thanks, especially to my husband, David Bunce, for not only encouraging me, but for remaining my biggest supporter and fan throughout our crazy life together.

Contents

FOREWORD

Liminal ['li-mə-nᵉl] *adjective*, of, relating to, or being an intermediate state, phase, or condition: in-between, transitional.

I BEGAN TO NOTICE SUBTLE CHANGES IN THE FACE OF THE STATUE. It appeared to morph from one face into another at an ever-increasing speed. I held my blowing hair with both hands to see more clearly as one after another female face appeared on the statue. Something obscure continued to block my view as if unseen fingers or long shadows flitted through my field of vision.

The faces became illuminated as they changed again and again until it seemed like a thousand women flashed before my eyes. At last, the vision ceased abruptly, and I stood alone gazing into the stone face of a mysterious woman. Maybe from her, or from someplace inside my head, or perhaps the depths of the universe itself, I heard a low pitched androgynous voice declare:

There will be three.

Before I could talk, I experienced realities beyond the physical world. The *veil* in my childhood home had grown remarkably permeable, allowing multiple spirits to interact with my family and me throughout my early, formative years. As my young brain grew, I developed schemas for both the physical world and the world that lies beyond the veil.

The summer of my tenth year we moved away from our haunted house into a more peaceful home. There my family began to openly discuss our shared hauntings. Realizing that we all had experienced the spirits validated my understanding of the nature of the world in its entirety, both corporeal and intangible.

What follows in these pages are experiences that advanced my understanding of the world just beyond what we see with our eyes. Like a world teeming with life just beyond the cedar leaves, just beyond the edge of the forest, I learned to observe the unseen within and beyond the veil.

As I grew older, many unusual circumstances propelled me on my path to becoming a gatekeeper, one who holds a key to unlock realities beyond the obvious. In the following pages, I will tell about some of those guiding encounters and how they helped me form a greater understanding of the wholeness of reality. These are true stories, however fantastic they may seem. Each of the events I share here is part of my own life's story, part of my path, the curious discoveries revealing the fullness of reality as I continue my journey, openhearted, toward the gate.

CHAPTER 1: TRANQUIL

[traŋ-kwəl] *adjective*, free from agitation of mind or spirit.

AFTER SPENDING A DECADE RENTING my great-grandmother's extremely haunted house in Chicago, Mom and Dad found a new home in the suburbs to call our own. At this time, we had seven kids with another on the way. Though I felt sad about leaving my old neighborhood and friends behind, I looked forward to moving into a bright, spacious home with a huge backyard and a creek running behind it.

Aunts, uncles, cousins, and all of us kids pitched in for the enormous task of cleaning, packing, and moving all our things to the new house. Dad's Uncle Gerald and his young family would follow us, occupying the house that had served as home to four generations of my family. This meant we did not have to empty the attic of trunks filled with nearly a century of photographs, archives, and documents, saving ourselves countless more hours of work.

Mom assigned rooms and roommates to fill the many bedrooms along a narrow hallway upstairs. She and Dad took the master bedroom at the top of the stairs. I recall the echoed shouts of delight as we scurried to our new rooms.

That first day ended with bags of MacDonald's hamburgers that Grammie Ethel and Gramps carried into the disheveled living room. I remember going to MacDonald's with Gramps one time and seeing the confused expression on the pimple-faced kid in a striped shirt when Gramps ordered his hamburger "rare."

We sat on the living room floor amid boxes and randomly placed furniture devouring hamburgers and grabbing handfuls of fries that had been poured out on a plate on the coffee table. Gramps even brought in cardboard trays filled with paper cups of Coca-Cola for us to drink, a rare treat that we all enjoyed.

After eating our fill, we carried heavy, green, army surplus duffle bags, stuffed with our clothes, upstairs to our rooms. We needed to sort our clothes to find pajamas for the night and clean clothes for the next day.

My sister Kate and I shared the second room from the stairs. We dumped the duffle on one of the unmade beds and began to sort and stack items into our drawers. Kate and I had shared a room in the old house as well. However, this one felt vastly different. It was bigger, lighter, and peaceful. We worked with the closet door wide open, something we would never have considered in our former home. There the closet held terrible and frightening things. We obsessively made sure the door clicked firmly shut whenever we spent time there.

In our new room, we had no such feelings or compulsions. It felt light and inviting. We each chose which side of the closet would be "ours," then left the door open even after finishing hanging up our clothes. As we completed putting things away, Mom came in with sheets and bedding for our twin beds. We would not sleep in the same double bed, but each have our own. At first, the thought of not having my sister's body as protection from whatever troubled us nightly in our old house gave me pause. We arranged the room by pushing our beds against different walls so that we each had only one side facing the open room.

This, I thought, *would give me some protection, especially if I faced outward with my back against the wall.*

Every night since my earliest memory, something lurked in the hallway of the old house and insinuated itself into our rooms at night. It would touch our hands, neck, or hair unless we had our bodies safely tucked under covers. If we slept with our backs turned toward the empty room, something would tickle our backs. For this reason, Kate and I had practiced scooting to the middle of the bed, back-to-back, and tucked way down in the sheets or covers to avoid exposure. Sleeping alone would not offer this protection. It made me anxious.

Still, Kate and I made up our beds, then sat on them, chatting and imagining how we might decorate our very own room. As we talked and giggled, I noticed that I felt no foreboding. The room seemed empty, save for the two of us and our things. Sitting-cross legged and bouncing slightly on my bed listening to Kate, I overheard happy conversations coming from other rooms. I heard my parent's voices downstairs. We had separated. We did not all rush from the tasks in our bedrooms back to the common areas for safety. For the first time in my life I felt safe in my own room in my own home.

At the time, I remained oblivious as to the reason for this new, safe, comfortable feeling. When Mom came to the door to tell us that it was time to go to bed, I noticed the empty duffle bags laying on the floor in front of the open closet.

"Should I clear out in front of the closet and close the door before bed?" I asked Kate as she tucked in.

"Nah," she said smiling, "I think it's alright."

Mom returned to kiss us goodnight,

"Sleep tight," she said, "Don't let the bedbugs bite."

She turned off the light asking, "Door open or closed?"

Before I could answer, Kate piped up, "Closed."

In the old house, we had to keep the bedroom door open to watch for spirits who frequented the hall. We had to make sure they passed before we could get up if we needed to use the bathroom during the night. A closed door meant we could not see what might lurk on the other side, leaving us vulnerable and unprepared.

Knowing this, I still said nothing—deferring to my older sister. I tucked in as safely as I could in the dark room with the hallway door closed and the closet door opened for the very first time in my life.

I awoke in the morning with my arm and one foot outside the covers. At first I quickly pulled them in, then realized that I had slept the whole night without incident. I glanced over to see Kate sleeping while facing the wall. I felt surprised that I had no fear. The house lay quiet. So quiet. The only sounds came from birds outside. I sensed no unseen energy filling the space. It felt empty, like when I spent the night at Grammie Ethel's house.

Not wanting to wake my sister I slipped out of bed, opened the door without anxiety, and tiptoed down the hall to the stairs. I did not feel anything looming behind me. I did not feel a need to stop at the top of the stairs to make sure I would not run into something unexpected. I just quietly made my way all alone downstairs and into the kitchen.

Mom sat at the kitchen table with her hands wrapped around a cup of coffee.

She looked up and smiled, her warm, green eyes shining.

"Good mornin' darlin,'" she smiled, "How'd you sleep?"

Mom asked this question every morning, but this morning it seemed particularly poignant.

Pulling up a chair, I sat next to her. "I slept GREAT!" I exclaimed. "I can't believe how well I slept."

I paused taking in the warm, light, welcoming energy of the new house. "It's so quiet here. Why do you think it's so much quieter here?"

She sipped her coffee. "I don't know, maybe because we aren't so close to a busy street, or as close to neighbors?"

"No," I said, "I mean, the house itself feels just so quiet."

She nodded, taking another sip.

"I love it here." I said. Our eyes met.

"Me too." Mom replied, "I don't think we are the only ones either," she looked at the clock on the stove, "It's after 9:00, and you and I are the only ones awake. The little ones aren't even up, and they usually are starving at the crack of dawn."

Just then, we began to hear the sounds of others making their way to the kitchen. Before long, it filled with happy, well-rested children clamoring for cereal.

Dad was the last to join us. Mom heaved her pregnant body out of her chair to kiss him and pour him a cup of coffee.

"Jesus!" He said, "Look at the time! I don't think I've ever slept this late."

Children made room for him at the kitchen table. We all sat or stood in that bright kitchen, talking excitedly about how much we loved the new house, how it felt so good, quiet, and tranquil.

CHAPTER 2: ADAPTATION

[a-dap-'tā-shən] *noun*, adjustment to environmental conditions: such as adjustment of a sense organ to the intensity or quality of stimulation.

WE MOVED INTO OUR NEW HOUSE IN LATE SUMMER. Any time not spent helping settle in found us exploring our backyard, the creek, and the park on the other side of the creek. Our new neighborhood sported vast yards with no fences. We quickly made friends with other children in the neighborhood, organizing group games of Kick The Can, Wiffle Ball, and elaborate games of Hide And Seek. We spent every hour outdoors, unsupervised and feral.

Mom had an antique school bell that she rang to call us in for chores or supper. We had to check in when the streetlights went on, but would often get permission to continue our play after dark if we stayed in the yard.

As summer waned, my anxiety about school rose. I had to begin a new year in a new school within a culture I did not know. I hated school. I suffered from trauma because humiliation and fear were the corner-stones of classroom management for my former school teachers in the city. I learned that by refusing to speak or participate in the large classes, I could render myself mostly invisible, and thus not a target. I tried to disappear behind my mother and my other siblings when we attended the open house prior to the school year. It did not work.

The principal did not appear scary in the slightest. With a kind face and a gentle voice, she praised my father and his work in the United States Attorney's office. She smiled at my siblings and me, declaring that we were such a beautiful family. I wondered if she would say such a thing if Mom were not there.

When I met my new teacher, I carefully sized him up. I knew I could not trust teachers. I had learned that they behaved one way around parents and other adults, and another way altogether in their classrooms. He asked me questions to which I gave no response. He appeared tall and thin, and dressed in the latest fashion. He wore dark-rimmed glasses, and reminded me of some men on TV sitcoms. He seemed nice enough, and yet I did not let my guard down.

The modern one-story building with large classrooms, flexible furniture, and broad windows stood in stark contrast to the multi-story brick dinosaur of a school building I had attended previously. The bright decorations on large bulletin boards in rooms and hallways were a far cry from the drab institutional green, vacant walls I had known.

As we made our way from classroom to classroom, I noticed other families. All the other children looked clean and pressed in new clothes and shoes. Since we had just experienced the cost of moving, my siblings and I wore the same school shoes and clothes from the previous spring. I recall a small group of girls dressed in the latest mod 1960s fashions, eyeing our faded and out-of-date clothing disdainfully. I hoped that I would not have to share a classroom with them.

I had trouble falling asleep the night before the first day of school, tossing and turning in my bed for what seemed like hours. The house lay perfectly still. My family all slept peacefully in that quiet house. A cool breeze wafted through the open windows. I heard cicadas singing outside in the giant oak tree, and from the hedgerow between our house and the neighbor's. It felt strange to find myself awake and not afraid. I thought about our old house and how terrifying things lurked in the shadows every single night. Nothing lurked here, and yet my anxiety kept me from rest.

I realized that I had not done spirit travel since we moved. I had learned from my guardian angel how to leave my body sleeping in bed and remove my conscious self to another place to avoid interaction with the many spirits who dwelt in my old house. In this house I felt no need to leave since no spirits haunted my nights. I knew, however, that my body needed rest, and decided to leave it so that,even if my mind couldn't, my body could rest.

Turning over to lie on my back I closed my eyes, letting my hands fall limply to my sides. First focusing on my breath, then, with each exhale, I visualized my energy lifting ever so slightly off my body. I could feel it return as I inhaled. With each new breath I pushed my energy further out and upward, continuing this process until my energy no longer reentered my body as I inhaled, but floated a few feet above my physical body. With my next exhale I gave control to my conscious spirit-self outside of my physical self and used the breath to lift me higher and higher until I found myself upright just outside the windows.

I had never spirit-traveled in this place, so I turned to see what I could see. In the astral dimension everything appears lit with a soft amber glow from which no shadow is cast, but even the most minute detail becomes acutely visible. One feels no temperature variation, no breeze, or wetness from rain or snow. Without a body, those stimuli are rendered mute. Only the immediacy and detail of the space—and one's relation to it—matter, and even those remain pliable.

I floated around the outside of my house, exploring the upper branches of the massive oak that loomed over the backyard. From there I noticed the stump of another oak nearby. I felt a connection to and between those trees and realized that they had grown old together. I sensed the loss that the living tree experienced when her sister fell.

I rose higher in the sky and noticed the rooftops of my neighborhood. No cars passed on the streets in this sleepy suburban town. I looked around for anybody else exploring the village in this reality but found myself alone. Drifting toward the school, I explored the playground and playing fields, floating, dancing, and soaring until I heard Mom's voice in the distance calling for us to wake up.

Inhaling sharply, I felt myself fall into my body with a start and jerked awake.

"Mom's been calling," Kate was already dressed, "You were dead to the world. What did you dream about?"

"Flying," I replied, pulling off the covers and setting my feet on the floor. I quickly got dressed and headed downstairs.

The kitchen bustled with many children eating cereal and getting ready for the first day of school. We all made bologna and mustard sandwiches for our lunches. Mom gave us each an apple, and a dime to buy milk. We packed it all in small brown paper bags, grabbed our new pencil cases filled with supplies, along with our binders of fresh loose-leaf paper, and set out for school.

We laughed, played tag, and rough-housed our way down the street, joining other neighborhood kids for the three-block walk to school. With several minutes to spare we played on the large, well-equipped playground. I glanced up recalling my bird's eye view from my travels the night before and wished I could just fly away again.

Just then, the bell rang. Children raced for the entrance doors. Nobody lined up. In my school in the city, we had to form straight, silent lines before the monitors let us enter the building. Sometimes when it rained, I recall them standing on the covered portico chatting as we stood shivering and drenched below them. In my new school, however, children raced directly into the building laughing and chatting. Smiling adults waited in the hallways to welcome the students.

I found my way to my fifth grade classroom, where my teacher waited at the door. I cast my eyes down as he held out his hand to shake mine.

"Welcome, Miss Schippers," he said. "Find the desk with your name on it, and have a seat."

I noticed that the group of girls I had seen at the open house sat together across the room, looking at me and whispering as they snickered. I set my things on my desk, adjusted my pale pink cat-eye glasses, smoothed out the plaid skirt of my dress, and faced the front of the room nervously.

Mr. U., as he wanted us to address him, informed us that we would start with a game to get to know one another. My heart beat faster as he said we would need to get up out of our seats and find one other person to learn about in order to introduce them to the rest of the class. Though I made friends easily in my neighborhood and among the safety of my siblings, school had always proved threatening and dangerous to me. Activities that forced me to initiate interactions with other children at school made me extremely anxious. I stood up with my head down looking around the room over the top of my eyes as children leaped from their seats, running to pick their favorite to interview. I quickly counted, hoping the class did not have an odd number of students knowing the humiliation that would follow if the teacher had to force a pair to accept me.

As I stood motionless, counting, I felt a light tap on my shoulder. Turning, I saw another little girl wearing a dress similar to mine. All the other girls wore hip-hugger miniskirts with wide belts and poorboy tops. Some even wore go-go boots. Our dresses buttoned in the back and had flared skirts. We both wore knee socks and dress shoes. My sister passed her old shoes down to me when she grew out of them. Though neat, clean, and pressed, we looked more like the little girls in an out-dated primer, than the other girls in the class.

"Hi, my name is Gail; what's yours?"

Surprised at my good fortune, I blurted out my name. I told her about just moving, and where I lived, discovering that she lived not too far from me. I told her about my big family, and learned that she had a small family. Gail seemed kind, and quiet like me. She invited me to eat lunch with her in the lunchroom. I agreed.

When the time came to introduce each other, Gail stood up and spoke clearly to the class, telling all she had learned about me, as the others watched suspiciously. When my turn came, I stood looking at the floor. I had not spoken in school for years, and I had not found a school voice. I wanted to introduce Gail because she showed me such kindness, but I could not raise my voice above a stuttering whisper. My face flushed, and my hands trembled. After years mastering the art of rendering myself invisible in the crowded classrooms in the city, I now stood, fully exposed in a light, spacious, uncrowded classroom with all eyes directed at me.

Gail, in an attempt to rescue me, jumped up and said her name and a few things about herself. Mr. U, did not approve.

"Thank you," he said coldly, "but we need her to tell us."

She sat back down, frustrated in her rescue. Some children began to whisper and giggle. Mr. U. did not stop them or grant me any grace. He sat at his desk for what felt like an eternity tapping his pencil impatiently.

I retreated further and further inward until I could almost not hear the murmurs and snickers. Looking at the tips of my shoes, I noticed one knee sock had slumped halfway down my calf. I noticed the pattern of the tile on the classroom floor and the small scuff mark on my left shoe. I heard my heart beating, and focused on maintaining even breaths.

"Miss Schippers!" I heard Mr. U. shout toward me. "You might as well just sit down if you have nothing to offer."

Nothing to offer, I agreed. *Nothing to offer.*

I remembered how I had made a commitment to selective mutism in school in third grade.

Mrs. Southern, my third-grade teacher, was cold and cruel. She had extremely stringent rules, and meted out swift and painful punishment to any child who violated one. She had a wooden ruler with a metal edge. If a child had dirty hands or fingernails, she would smack them across the knuckles with that metal edge, leaving painful bruises. When not sitting at her desk looking at movie magazines, she would walk up and down the long rows of desks tapping that ruler on the palm of her hand. If children slouched in their seats she would grab the hair at the nape of their neck and yank so hard that it left hairs in her fingers.

●ᵃ˙ᵛ˙⋯˙⋮⋯●

One chilly day in October, we had come in from the schoolyard after lunch. For my birthday Uncle Jack had given me my very own hardcover chapter book that I adored. My father had many books in his personal library to which I had free access, along, of course, with the public library, but I had never *owned* a book Dad gave me a book plate to secure inside the front cover designating it as my very own property. I loved to read. I loved the brightly colored shiny cover of *Rebecca Of Sunnybrook Farm* by Kate Douglas Wiggins. I took it out to recess to read, but had to stop at a particularly exciting part when the bell rang.

●ᵃ˙ᵛ˙⋯˙⋮⋯●

Returning to the classroom I dutifully stowed it away inside my desk as Mrs. Southern passed out arithmetic papers. She had scheduled 45 minutes for arithmetic right after lunch. My legs and nose still felt cold as I took the stack of papers from the student seated directly in front of me, peeled off a mimeographed copy, and passed the rest behind me. To my delight the paper had about sixty two- and three-digit mixed addition and subtraction problems without regrouping. After sniffing the purple print, I set to work. I loved arithmetic because once you knew it, you knew it. No guessing, just clear predictable answers.

●ᵃ˙ᵛ˙⋯˙⋮⋯●

Writing my name in the space at the top of the page I set to work. Finishing quickly, I glanced at the clock on the wall above Mrs. Southern. Only ten minutes had passed. Noticing that Denise to my left had finished the first row, and Joey to my right had only finished the first problem, I looked to Mrs. Southern for a cue as to what to do next. She grew angry when other children raised their hand to declare that they had finished, so I knew I should not do that.

In my house, boredom was not acceptable. "If in doubt," Mom and Dad would say, "read."

Mrs. Southern licked her finger to turn the magazine page as I stealthily lifted the top of my desk, removed my book, and began reading silently.

Everyone startled at a loud *smack*, followed by my name screamed from the front of the room.

"What are you doing?!" she screeched.

Stammering, I replied meekly, "I'm reading ma'am."

"It's not reading time! It's arithmetic time! Get to your arithmetic!"

"I finished." I declared quietly.

She craned her neck to turn to see the clock, then looked back at me menacingly.

"You rushed! You could not have done them all in that amount of time."

I held up my paper to show the completed work.

Well you couldn't have done a good job. Check your answers!"

"Yes ma'am." I said stowing my book once again inside my desk.

I knew that checking answers meant doing the operations in reverse from the bottom up, so to keep it interesting for myself I started in the bottom right corner of the page and worked my way to the top. Before long, with all answers checked, I felt confident that I had completed my task. Only ten more minutes had passed. Now Denise had finished four rows, and Joey had finished four problems.

I should've known better than to take out my book again. I should've known that it would infuriate Mrs. Southern, but I didn't. I could not imagine angering someone, especially a teacher, for reading, and so, once again, I quietly opened my desk, slipped my book out, and held it in my hands happily anticipating a solid twenty minutes of uninterrupted reading before arithmetic time ended.

It must've been an especially engaging part of the story because I did not notice Mrs. Southern bearing down on me until it was too late. She grabbed the top of my book and violently yanked it out of my hands. Instinctively I gripped the part I held and the beautiful front cover separated from the rest with a sickening sound that tore not only the book, but my poor little heart as well. She snatched the rest of my book from my limp hands, and stomped back to the front of the room.

Every eye shifted back and forth from Mrs. Southern to me. I felt my own eyes stinging with fury as she carelessly tossed my treasure on the corner of her desk so that the lovely ruined cover dropped with a clang into the metal trash bin beside it.

Mrs. Southern returned to her desk chair saying, "I told you it was arithmetic time."

"I finished!" I hissed through my clenched teeth.

"I told you to check your answers." she replied with growing annoyance.

"I. Checked. My. Answers." I growled with my eyes squeezed into the fiercest glare I could muster.

Mrs. Southern had had enough, "Bring your paper to my desk! If you have even one incorrect answer, you are going to the Disciplinarian's office!"

An audible gasp filled the room as every child's eyes widened. The disciplinarian had an office next to the principal. We all knew that In that office, on the wall, hung a large paddle for beating bad children. They watched with horror as I furiously grabbed my paper and walked slowly and steadily to her desk, glaring at my cruel teacher. She held out her hand for it, but I dropped it on top of the movie magazine sitting on her desk. She did not miss the irony of my deliberate gesture and frowned even more.

My classmates barely breathed as she took the red pencil from the cup on her desk. As she went from one problem to the next, I glanced down at my ruined book on her desk and the separated cover in her trash. While my classmates held their breath in fear for the fate that lay before me, I felt nothing but pure rage.

"Well," she said dismissively, after finding that I had answered every problem correctly, "I told you it was arithmetic time." She avoided eye contact as I glared unflinchingly. "Go back to your seat and sit there... and I don't want to hear a peep out of you!"

I would not give her, or the others, the satisfaction of letting the tears that welled up in my eyes fall. I returned to my seat seething with more fury than I had ever seen or felt. I sat in my chair, squeezed my hands together on the desktop, and continued to shoot rage from my eyes directly at Mrs. Southern. She noticed, nervously put her magazine in her drawer, and began shuffling papers on her desk. I did not look away. I did not move a muscle. Not a peep came out of me, but the depth of my fury flooded from every cell in my being.

I did not move to turn around when the boy behind me smacked the stack of papers on my back to pass forward. I did not move when the next stack of papers came to my desk. I sat with hands folded, not flinching and not making a sound for the remainder of the day. I went home without my book, but told nobody what had happened.

The next day I again took my seat and refused to move or make a sound. I continued this day after day, spending every minute in the classroom glaring at Mrs. Southern without a sound. I stopped doing work. I stopped interacting with other children. I just sat there feeding the wild beast of my fury. Mrs. Southern never contacted my parents as I began failing every subject. I simply refused to participate. I did as I had been told. I sat there without a peep. Before long Mrs. Southern moved me to the back corner of the room where she didn't have to feel my angry eyes on her. Each morning when all the other children dutifully held out their hands for inspection, she walked right past me ignoring the fact that I refused to hold out my hands. With each passing day, I became more and more comfortable in my silence. Soon I began spending every day at school inside my own imagination, removed from the world around me, much the same way I left my body unattended in my bed at night inside the walls of my spirit-infested home. I learned how to become invisible and maintained that invisibility and mutism at school for five years.

···

Nothing to offer, I thought. *Nothing to offer.*

Mr. U. had met my expectations. Though so much about my new school appeared different, some things remained the same. I began another school year in mute non-participation.

Chapter 3: Pariah

[pə-'rī-ə] *noun*; one that is despised or rejected

For reasons unknown to me, my big brother Dave went to the neighborhood Catholic School while the rest of us attended the public school. Fortunately, most of the kids in the neighborhood also attended the Catholic school. Attending a different school provided a protective arena for play in my neighborhood saving me from the reputation I quickly acquired at school.

After school and on weekends, I remained my playful and engaging self, but when the school bell rang I retreated into silent endurance. My mute non-participation must have frustrated my teacher to no end. It also brought out a heightened level of cruelty in my classmates. Becoming the butt of many taunts, I mentally removed myself from that space and immersed myself in my Egyptian studies.

Since my youngest days growing up amid spirits, I sought knowledge of all manner of mysticism, hoping to understand the unseen world that I had experienced. Anthropology and history had always fascinated me as well. My father's engaging stories of the past piqued my interest and curiosity. I studied ancient mythology and magic from a wide variety of cultures. Ancient Egypt, in particular, grabbed my imagination. I began studying classical Egyptology and ancient Egyptian language at an early age. Dad nurtured my interest, bringing me countless books on the subject which I devoured voraciously. By age eight I yearned to study ancient Egyptian hieroglyphics. I loved laboring over the mysterious and beautiful writing and attempted to copy some of the artwork and hiero-glyphics I saw.

Dad and I shared this interest, so one day, he took me to The Oriental Institute at The University of Chicago, a museum that special-izes in ancient Near East cultures. I remember walking through the exhibits in awe of the abundance of artifacts. Standing gobsmacked in front of an enormous sculpture of Amenhotep, I gazed in respectful silence at the remains of an unknown mummy from thousands of years ago. To my great delight, my father told me that I could pick out a book from the gift shop. Perusing the shelves, I searched for something special. I asked the clerk if she knew of a book that a child my age could read to learn the ancient Egyptian language of the eighteenth dynasty, or the classical hieroglyphic era.

The clerk smiled, then pointed me to a picture book of simple phonetic hieroglyphics that a child might use to write their name, or other words using the basic phonetic symbols. I looked at it briefly, then told her that I thought I should probably first learn the language before learning the script.

Apparently, my pigtailed eight-year-old self surprised her. She asked me a few more questions, which I answered with conviction. Next, she looked in amazement at my father, standing mute and proud.

"Just a minute," she said. "Can you wait right here? I need to talk to somebody."

After a few short minutes, she returned, asking us to follow her to the third floor. There I met Dr. Livingood, the chair of the ancient languages department at The University of Chicago. Mountains of papers and texts overflowed the shelves behind her cluttered desk. Her blue eyes twinkled beneath a crown of soft white curls. Her broad and friendly smile appeared as we entered her office.

"Well, well," she said, "Who have we here?"

The clerk explained that I was the child who inquired about a book to learn the 18th dynasty Egyptian language. Professor Livingood asked why I wanted to study that, and I told her that I wanted to be able to read the papyruses for myself. I told her that I wanted to translate the ancient texts that might one day lead me to the burial place of Hatshepsut, the famous female pharaoh from the late eighteenth dynasty.

She smiled attentively as I went on. I told her I shared a nickname with Amenhotep III's chief wife. I explained how I saw Queen Tiyi as a role model since she was known to be a musician, scribe, and well-educated queen. I told her that I knew the way I spelled and pronounced my name differed from the German translation that used an "e" instead of "i" in the last syllable.

Professor Livingood's warm smile transitioned into an expression of gleeful amazement.

"I think maybe I can help you," she said.

Professor Livingood gifted me with an enormous graduate-level reference book that Dad had to carry due to its massive size. She instructed me to read the introduction and the first chapters that explained how the writing combined phonetics as well as pictographs. She told me that I might find it confusing, but that even Jean-Francois Champollion did at first, too. Then she asked me if I knew of whom she spoke. I nodded, eagerly telling her that I knew Champollion transliterated the Egyptian part of the Rosetta Stone, breaking the key to the mysterious writing. Smiling broadly, Professor Livingood gave me her phone number, saying to call if I needed help, and to call when I had completed those first chapters so we could make an appointment to come back for another visit.

I couldn't wait to begin. I dove into the text, excluding all else. Dad helped me find definitions of English words I hadn't yet learned. In a few months, I was ready to return. Professor Livingood asked me questions about what I had read, then continued to guide me through the introductory chapters. When it got to actually learning the language, it seemed oddly comfortable, even familiar. Sometimes during our visits, Professor Livingood took me into the bowels of the museum to see where graduate students and assistants labored over tiny shards of pottery and scrolls of hieroglyphs. She introduced me to the archaeologists there as her youngest Egyptology student. I loved not only the attention but also the recognition as a capable scholar.

I dared not bring my precious books to school due to the trauma of losing the first book I owned to my third-grade teacher, so I visualized the lessons from the text, and scribbled tiny hieroglyphics in the margins of textbooks, and the edges of papers. This gave the appearance of working on classwork, thereby avoiding my teacher's scrutiny from his desk in the front of the room. He rarely sat in his chair, but perched on the edge of his desk with one leg on the floor. He flirted with the popular girls, and treated the popular boys as buddies. I looked at him with disdain as he laughed and teased with them, ignoring the less popular kids.

I never spoke, nor did the assigned work. I did not look like or behave like my classmates, so I soon became a pariah.

I ate lunch alone with my head down, avoiding unnecessary contact. I could hear them talking about me and calling me cruel, disgusting names. Sometimes, Gail would swing with me on the playground, but mostly I preferred to spend time alone.

I became the target of small stones, then snowballs during winter. Sometimes kids followed me home, pelting me with snowballs. Trying to avoid them one day, I took a different route home from school. Though longer, it brought me close to the route my big brother took from his school. Still, they followed. I ran as fast as I could, with them gaining on me, shouting obscenities. At last, I saw Dave and his friends approaching. I turned and ran toward them. The boys that followed me had no idea that I was running toward safety for me and danger for them.

As soon as Dave realized what was happening, he and three friends, older than the boys who chased me, began to run toward me, picking up and packing snowballs of their own. They chased those kids for blocks, pelting them with hard-packed missiles until they dispersed into their own homes.

Relieved, I made my way toward home as Dave and his friends caught up.

"What's going on?" he asked.

"They do this every day," I replied, "I don't walk home with the little kids because I don't want them to have to deal with it."

"Don't worry," The boys assured me, "Walk this way home every day. We will take care of those little bastards."

Though my walks home from school became peaceful, even fun with my brother's charming friends, cruelty ramped up at school and even began to bleed into the classroom, with Mr. U. joining in.

"What are you doing back there?" Mr. U. stood up from his perch on his desk.

At first, I didn't realize that he was speaking to me. Then I noticed him approaching. I tried to obscure the paper on my desk covered with minute hieroglyphics and tiny drawings with both arms and looked down.

"Are you working on the assignment?" he said, turning to smirk at the rest of the class, "Because you haven't done a single assignment since you started occupying space in that desk."

Several children chuckled. "What are you doing back here?"

He pulled the paper out from under my arms and displayed what looked like scribblings to the class. They cackled and howled while he returned to the front of the room as my face grew crimson.

Though no one in that class had ever heard me speak, still looking down at my hands, I said, "*Yeh wek Heh Bek.*"

He spun around, shocked, and said, "What did you say?"

I looked him squarely in the eye and repeated loudly, "*Yeh wek Heh Bek!*"

He grew angry as kids chuckled, then fell silent, noticing his growing rage.

"What does that mean?" he demanded.

Then I spoke the only other words I would utter in his class forever.

"Look it up," I said.

Dad had told me that the best insults are the ones where the recipient has no idea they had been insulted, but you do. Mr. U. grew livid. I had never seen him angry like that. He pointed to the door and screamed, "GET OUT!"

Not sure if I could move past him safely, I remained seated glaring at him.

"GET OUT!" he repeated, "Go to the principal's office. I am going to speak to your father."

Mr. U. had used the ultimate threat. Fathers worked. To disturb one's father meant inconvenience and probably a more severe punishment. I stood feeling oddly satisfied, gathered my things from my desk, and walked slowly out the door, down the hall to the principal's office.

The school secretary had a pretty face and a warm, friendly nature. "Having a little trouble in class are we?" she asked. "Have a seat there. Miss D. will see you soon."

I sat silently in the chair facing the secretary's desk with a large glass window to the corridor behind me. After several minutes, Mr. U. stormed into the office. He did not even look in my direction but went straight into the principal's office. I heard them talking. I heard *insubordination*, *refusal* to do anything, *trouble-maker*, and *disturbed* from him. Then it got quiet. He emerged, again not even glancing in my direction, and stormed out of the office. Then Miss D. called me in.

She motioned to the chair in front of her desk as she took a seat. I sat down nervous, but self-righteous.

"Mr. U. is very upset. He says you swore at him in class."

My head shot up, and I looked directly at her. "I did no such thing" I said.

"He says you swore in a foreign language."

"I did not." I repeated.

"He says you threatened his authority in his class."

"What authority?" I said under my breath.

"Well," she went on, "He will not let you back in class until we can make an appointment for a conference with both your mom and dad. I'm going to have to call your dad at work."

She studied my face. I did not fear Mom or Dad's reaction. I felt sorry that he would have to miss work, and that mom would have to find somebody to watch the little kids at home, but I felt justified in my response to his bullying.

I nodded as she picked up the phone.

"You will need to stay here until the end of the day, then stay home until we can meet. Do you understand?"

I nodded again. "Okay, wait in the chair in the outside office, please so I can call your mom and dad. Do you have a book to read?"

I felt great relief that I did not have to return to my class, though I did not relish having to sit on display in the office for the remainder of the day. I did not have a book, so instead, I again retreated into my imagination until the bell rang. I waited to be dismissed after all the other children had left, and walked unaccosted all the way home.

Mom did not scold me when I got home. I found her in the kitchen over the stove.

"What happened in school?" she said, stirring spaghetti sauce, "It's not like you to swear at your teacher." She knew I never spoke in school, that I avoided confrontation and that something must have driven me to extremes.

"I didn't, Mom. I promise. He just thought I did. He is so mean."

"Well," she smiled lovingly at me, "We are meeting tomorrow at 10:00, so you get to sleep in."

I loved her so much at that moment. She saw me. She believed me. My parents said that they would always trust our word if we never lied. I had always tried to be honest, even when it meant punishment. That commitment paid off now.

Dad didn't get home until after I had gone to bed. In the morning, though I did not sleep in, I did not have to get up with the others. Nobody talked to me about my dilemma. Not even my sister Kate, with whom I shared a bedroom, said a thing. It seemed to me that I might not get punished as everyone expected.

Three chairs stood together against one wall of the principal's office with two across from them. After shaking hands in greeting, I sat between my parents with my feet barely reaching the floor, and the principal seated opposite us. Mr. U. entered the room with great purpose and flare and, ignoring Mom, introduced himself to my father. They shook hands and then seated themselves. Mr. U. crossed his legs confidently.

"It seems that your daughter has displayed disrespect and insubordination toward her teacher," said the principal.

I saw love in Dad's eyes as he turned to look down at me and felt safe between my parents.

Miss D. went on, "Mr. U., would you like to explain to Mr. and Mrs. Schippers what happened?"

"I would indeed," he said with dramatic flair. "Your *daughter* refuses to participate in class. She refuses to do any work. She refuses to comply with even my simplest request. The final straw was that she cursed at me in front of the class. When I asked what she said she responded with more disrespect. How am I supposed to maintain order if a child can get away with such insubordination?!"

Dad looked to me as I shook my head.

"What did you say?" he asked.

"*Yeh wek Heh Bec.*" I said.

Dad's eyebrows shot up as he smiled broadly at me, knowing that what I had said to my teacher was, "*Thou art wont to be cool*" in the language of eighteenth dynasty Egypt.

"That's it!" Mr. U. pointed to me. "I asked her what it meant!"

"Did he ask you?" Dad said, turning from Mr. U. to me. I nodded. "Did you tell him?"

"No," I replied, "I told him to look it up."

Dad's delight became even more visible in his twinkling eyes as he turned back to my teacher and asked, "Did you?"

"What?" asked my teacher.

"Look it up?" Dad replied, clearly dominating the room.

Then he turned to me to ask why I would say he was trying to be cool? I told him my observations of his behavior along with the terrible taunting and bullying I had to endure every day in his class. I told about how he flirted with the pretty girls and made fun of the others like me. My father's discontent became more visible as he shot looks in the direction of my now squirming teacher.

Finally, Miss D. dismissed Mr. U. to return to his classroom. After he left, she asked me to wait in the outer office. Then she and my parents spoke for a long time.

I did not return to class when they emerged, but went out to lunch with Mom and Dad.

"What made you think of that?" Mom asked over hamburgers at The Village Inn.

"Dad always said that the best insults are the ones that go over the person's head. He always tells us to look it up when we don't know something, so I just did that."

"Dad smiled at Mom, then at me before he said, "You don't have to go back to his class." I looked at them confused. "You will have a new teacher on Monday. I'm not sending you back to be bullied by that worm."

"Dave!" Mom said.

That was it. On Monday, I moved to a new classroom. I remained mute and noncompliant, but began to see the school psychologist and other support personnel who hoped to help me with what troubled me. Nobody, however, asked why I didn't speak in school, and I didn't offer it, but at least people began to treat me with kindness, if not understanding.

CHAPTER 4: METAMORPHOSIS

[ˌme-tə-ˈmȯr-fə-səs] *noun*, change of form, structure, or substance.

IN SEVENTH GRADE, MY SELECTIVE MUTISM LANDED ME in a self-contained special education classroom located in the basement adjacent to the cafeteria at the junior high. I continued to refuse to speak or participate in schoolwork or the social aspects of junior high.

At lunch, in the corridors, and at study hall I remained the butt of many cruel jokes and taunts, but Miss Hennigan's class offered a safe harbor for most of the day. She often tried to include me but made no demands. She allowed me to maintain my dignity and my solitude.

I observed how she spoke with kindness and respect to other students and me. She told us about herself, how she lived in Old Town and loved folk music. Sometimes she played records. She smiled and laughed freely. I noticed that her demeanor did not change in or outside the presence of other adults. She only changed when defending one of her students. Then she became a mother lion. I liked and trusted her.

I had study hall for the last hour of the day in the cafeteria. Miss Hennigan never had to take study hall duty due to her caseload of troubled students. The study hall monitors did not care what the students worked on as long as they had noses in books. Having my own locker, I felt safe enough to bring my hieroglyphics workbook and text to school. I kept them in my locker just off the cafeteria. During study hall, I would find a seat far away from other students and work on my Ancient Egyptian studies.

One Friday, the study hall monitor got violently ill at the beginning of the period. Since all of Miss Hennigan's students had study hall that same hour, she stepped in to supervise. After watching the changeover across the cafeteria, I returned to my studies.

Suddenly someone pulled out the chair next to me. Panicked, I quickly covered my work as Miss Hennigan sat down.

"Whatcha doing there?" She asked, indicating the book and workbook that I slid cautiously away from her.

I shook my head, protecting my work with both arms. She just smiled tenderly, glancing from the books to my face.

"May I see?" She asked.

I knew I could say "no" and she would respect me, but I really trusted her. Nodding, I gently slid my workbook toward her so she could see my translations and transliterations of an ancient dead language from the Iron Age. Her eyes widened, and her mouth fell open.

"Wow!" She said, turning a few pages. "Just wow!"

She looked deeply into my eyes. "This is amazing!" Then she looked at more pages of hieroglyphics, shaking her head in disbelief.

"Wow!" She repeated, pointing to my head, "I just knew something wonderful was happening inside there. Why didn't you let me know you could do this?"

I shrugged.

"How long have you been working on this?"

"Since I was eight," I said quietly.

She had never heard the sound of my voice, but did not react.

"That's when you stopped speaking in school, right?"

I nodded again.

"Does this have anything to do with that?

"No." I told her, "Not this."

"What then?" She asked, "Why did you stop speaking in school? What happened?"

No one had ever asked me why. Teachers, counselors, and even my parents had never asked why I disassociated from school and the people there. Miss Hennigan asked, so I told her.

She listened without interruption as I told about Mrs. Southern, my book, her demand that she not hear a peep, and my decision to comply ... completely.

Miss Hennigan's face grew red. Her brow furrowed, and she shook her head.

"I'm so sorry." She said with genuine empathy, "Some people should be hung by their thumbs."

Then, without saying anything else, Miss Hennigan gently slid my workbook back in front of me and rose from her seat. Pushing in her chair, she gave me one nod, and with a proud smile, walked away to monitor the other students. I returned to my work.

On Monday, she did not make a big deal of our conversation. She did not expect me to say anything in class, but after the others began working, she sidled up next to me and whispered.

"It's okay to work on your hieroglyphics in here. You can go to your locker to get your books if you like."

Then she walked to the classroom door and opened it, smiling. I hesitated, then retrieved my workbook and text from my locker, and began working happily in my classroom.

After that, I spoke more to Miss Hennigan and the other children in the class. She asked me to show the other students how I could write in hieroglyphics. My classmates loved it and asked me to write their names in hieroglyphics. Miss Hennigan gave me index cards cut lengthwise. I wrote each child's name along with Miss Hennigan's, and she taped them to each desk.

Following that I began participating in other subjects in school, completing assignments that still left me time to continue my personal educational pursuits.

Miss Hennigan left the following year, but I never forgot how she took the time to really see, know, and honor me, and how that simple act of kindness helped ease the trauma I endured.

CHAPTER 5: CHRYSALIS

[kri-sə-ləs] *noun*, a sheltered state or stage of being or growth

THE WHOLE SUMMER BEFORE I TURNED FOURTEEN, I spent Up North at the lake. Since Dad had to stay in Chicago to work, Mom hired my younger sister, Annie, a friend, Janet, and myself as her "summer girls" to help with the younger children and take care of the house. Our new place had a small cement block summer house attached to what used to be a bait shop run by the former owners. It had one small bedroom, a tiny bathroom, and a living area with a small kitchen. We also had a record player and three records that we played repeatedly since we could not pick up a decent radio station way up in the north woods. We girls got to make it our own place, cooking our meals as we wished, and having lots of freedom after helping Mom with the chores and the little kids all day. Mom also hired Dave and two of his friends to help with groundskeeping and other "men's work" around the place. They transformed half of the garage into a really cool "hippie" bunkhouse with a Jamaican flag and other tapestries covering the walls.

We did chores for Mom during the day, then sang around a campfire at night. It felt like such a safe place to spend a summer with a small group of friends and family. We had cousins who also summered in the area, so we extended our group to include the older cousins. We also met some local kids and guys who worked at a boys' camp across the lake from my grandparents cabin.

I had just finished my freshman year at Saint Louise de Marillac

High School for young women. I felt safe and accepted there and began to thrive in the close-knit community under the guidance of the Daughters of Charity, a radical order of young nuns who participated in anti-war demonstrations on the weekends and helped us find our feminist power on weekdays.

Feeling the affirmation of new friends, and nothing but possibilities ahead, life took on a more open, positive tone.

On our day off, Janet, Annie, and I packed a backpack with bug spray, matches, water, and lunch and headed out for a hike along a wild river about a mile from our place. Intending to hike from one bridge to the next—about three miles as the crow flies—we set out in the late morning without a care.

The river ran slow and shallow in most spots but wound back and forth like a slithering snake. After a couple of hours, we came across a deeper hole and decided to stop for lunch and a swim. After that, we set out again, expecting to see the bridge around every bend in the river. Soon the banks became impassable. Broad marshy bogs bordered it on both sides for thousands of feet. We tried following thickets of trees for high ground but eventually had to walk in the river as it became swifter and deeper.

At one point, Annie lost her shoes in the mucky river bottom. We fashioned make-shift foot coverings out of both Janet's socks and mine with pieces of birch bark slid in-between. Hours passed without finding any sign of a crossing. Exhaustion set in, and we grew concerned as the sun reached the treetops. Reluctantly, coming to the realization that we would have to figure out how to spend the night out in the wilderness, we began looking for a patch of dry ground on the riverbank.

We found a flat, sandy spot with the river at our backs. Next we quickly searched for low-hanging dead or fallen wood, along with dried grass, small dry sticks, and pine cones to use for kindling, and built a small fire. We made sure we had enough wood to last the night, out of fear of bears, wolves, and any other dangerous creature that might lurk in that vast wilderness.

Thankful that our clothes had thoroughly dried after our swim and that the night air did not feel too chilly, we huddled close to our small fire and decided to take turns sleeping. One would close her eyes while the other two kept watch. Though thoroughly exhausted, not one of us could close our eyes. Instead, we sat by the fire listening to otters slide into the nearby river .

Before long, the wind picked up in the overhead trees, and we began to hear the low rumble of thunder in the distance.

"That's pretty far west of us," Annie said, answering the unasked question. "It will probably miss us."

Janet and I nodded hopefully, looking toward the starless sky.

"Of course, if we do get a storm," she went on matter of factly, "We will have to move up the bank in case there's a flash flood."

We hadn't considered a possible flood when choosing the site for our fire. We wanted the river at our backs, so we only had to keep vigil in one direction through the night. That logic resulted in our campsite on a low, sandy bank. Now the river itself posed a potential danger.

"We will be fine," I said, trying to convince myself as much as the others. "Let's sing."

We sang songs from the record albums we listened to every day, as well as new songs by Bob Dylan.

The wind picked up even more as the hours ticked by, and we added sticks to the dancing fire. At one point, between songs, I thought I heard the sound of voices. Shushing the others, we listened closely. It was Mom's voice, among others, calling our names! We all leapt to our feet and began shouting back in the direction of the voices. Then we stopped to listen again. The voices sounded further away, as if the searchers headed in the opposite direction.

"Build up the fire!" Janet suggested, "so they can see us!"

We began throwing wood on the fire, making the flames reach above our heads. Then we shouted again.

"This way! We are here!"

Then we waited but heard no reply.

"They're not going to find us tonight," Annie said. "They're going the wrong way. We are going to be here all night."

We looked at our reserves of firewood being consumed before our eyes. We had no flashlight and did not want to brave the pitfalls of the pitch dark woods to gather more. My heart sank as I contemplated the thought of waiting until daylight for rescue, or worse, to retrace our arduous steps home. Lightning began to flash, casting eerie, instantaneous shadows that made my imagination run wild. Imagined monsters appeared as tall looming figures in the trees. I talked myself out of alarm, chalking it up to pareidolia, and stood looking in the direction of last-heard voices.

At last, we heard familiar voices again, this time coming from a different direction! We all jumped to face them, shouting our location as loudly as possible. The sounds kept moving: first closer, then further away, then from a new direction altogether as the wind blew and lightning flashed, and the fire dwindled.

"Is there more than one rescue team?" Janet asked, "Maybe they are coming from different locations?"

"I don't know. I keep hearing Mom's voice. It's hard to miss!" I laughed nervously.

"It's the wind." said Annie, "making the sound seem to move. We will have to stay here and keep calling until they find us." Then, looking at the remnants of our fire, "Even if the fire goes out."

We called back and forth for more than an hour until our voices grew hoarse and sore. At long last, we made out lights moving in our direction, straight through the woods. We yelled furiously, then laughed with relief as Mom, Dave, his friends, and a tall man we did not know made their way to us.

Mom had called the forest ranger when we did not return by sunset. He told her that he could do nothing until daylight with the storm coming in, but would organize a search party for first light. Mom was not satisfied. She had no intention of waiting until morning to bring her chickens, as she called us, home. She drove to Otto's house and asked if he could help. Otto was a woodsman in his late eighties, bent from years of hard labor and smelling of the woods. She had known him since she was a little girl in the 1930s. He told her that her best chance was to get this other feller who knew every inch of the river. The feller, Otto said, did not have a phone, but Otto gave Mom directions to the man's cabin and told her to tell him that he sent her to ask for his help.

I do remember his story, but not his name. He lived alone in a rough cabin off a rutted two-track near the river. He fished and trapped every inch of the woods along the river, and knew it like the lines on his hand. Though it appeared he had been sleeping, he answered the door. He listened as Mom told him her predicament and that Otto had sent her. They waited outside, watching the flashes of lightning and roiling clouds of the approaching storm until he returned fully dressed. The woodsman began to ask questions: what time had we left? How tall and how physically fit were we? Then he contemplated. Mom said she imagined him picturing the river from where we stepped off the road and down the bank by the bridge.

He spoke to himself, saying, "They would've gotten hungry somewhere near the bend where the new yellow birch are comin' up." Then he addressed Mom, "What did they pack for lunch?"

"I'm not sure. Why?"

"I need to figure out how long they would've stopped."

"Probably a sandwich and maybe an apple or something," Mom replied, "They had a canteen of water, too."

"Okay," he mused, "They probably stopped to swim in the pool just before the hemlocks ..." Then, turning back toward Mom, he said, "If they kept going, they hit some pretty rough terrain. They would stop at dark, I suppose."

Mom nodded, knowing that we knew better than to try to make our way through rough terrain after dark.

"They know how to build a fire." Mom added, "I imagine they have matches."

"Alright then, I have a pretty good idea where to find them. You drive your car, and I'll take my truck."

Mom followed his ancient pickup in her station wagon along the sandy road. Then he turned off the road directly into the woods. Mom knew she could drive through pretty much anything, having learned to drive on the deep sand roads and two-tracks up north, still this terrain put her to the test.

Soon he just stopped his truck—near no landmarks that Mom could make out—and got out.

"You can wait here or follow, "he said, "I think I have a pretty good idea where they are."

Mom and the boys grabbed their flashlights, hopped out of the car, and followed the man into the woods. He carried no light, yet walked completely unimpeded deeper and deeper into the thick woods.

"We're gettin' close to the river," he said after walking for about thirty minutes, "You might want to call them so we can get right to them."

Though it seemed to us that their voices were nearby at first but then receded to a greater distance, Mom told us that they walked a straight line from the vehicles and reached the river about twenty feet from our location.

We felt overjoyed at the sight of our rescuers. Hugging our rescuers, in part to keep ourselves from crying, we were determined to prove our competence and courage. We explained our trek as we walked out of the woods, directly to the vehicles.

Streaks of purple appeared in the eastern sky as we arrived home at last. Annie and Janet took showers first to wash off the grime, sweat, and bug spray. I flopped on the couch, waiting my turn, but fell fast asleep before the shower freed up.

We didn't get into any trouble. Mom let us sleep late and have the next day off after our ordeal. Since the bathroom seemed constantly occupied, I decided to have a swim in the lake to "wash" up. Then I laid out on a towel, dozing as my skin air-dried.

A few weeks later we packed and closed up the place to return to the city. School would begin soon, and we had to get back to do everything needed to get ready. I no longer hated school the way I did before high school, and actually looked forward to seeing my school friends after a long summer, but I didn't feel particularly well. My body ached all the time. I felt a constant dull throbbing behind my eyes and had no appetite. I felt tired and run down.

This general malaise continued for the first several weeks of school, then I fell terribly ill, running a high fever for more than a week. My head felt as if it would split like a watermelon. I could not lift my head off the pillow, but the pressure of the pillow itself caused excruciating pain. My body trembled with chills and burned with heat. Sweat soaked my body, hair, and bed. I could barely swallow for the bulging glands in my neck. Mom moved the little boys out of their room off the living room and moved me in to keep a better eye on me. I needed her help to drag my aching body to the toilet.

I remember Mom cradling my head with one hand and stripping the soaked pillowcase from my pillow, replacing it with a cool, clean one. Each day I grew weaker with the relentless fever and pain. I became delirious seeing terrifying dark things hovering in the upper corners of the room. I did not have the strength to make them leave and couldn't make Mom understand how they tormented me.

I remember short visits from worried friends, Johnny and Moose came to call, but I did not make good company. The pain and fever made conversation impossible, so they just sat in a chair nearby for a few minutes, then left. I think I recall Johnny putting a cool cloth on my forehead, but I could not be sure I did not dream it.

When conscious, I tried to lay as still as possible since every tiny movement brought waves of pain. One afternoon I listened to the voices of the little kids playing in the living room, and a TV in the distance. I just hurt so much, I desperately wanted to escape. I thought of separating my spirit from my sick body just for some momentary relief, but as I began lifting off the bed, those terrifying black things in the corners took notice. I quickly fell back into my body, afraid that if I tried spirit travel, my body might die. I did not want to die. I only wanted to get some relief.

In my fevered thinking, I imagined that if I just hovered directly over my physical body, I could keep tabs on my surroundings, and not leave for good. The black things still scared me, but I thought that I could drop quickly into myself if they moved suddenly toward me. Painfully, I turned onto my back, feeling the weight of my head pressing on the damp pillow. Keeping my eyes closed with my hands to my side, I focused on the spot between my eyes, watching for the light tunnel to appear.

At first, I saw a purple dot that began to undulate. Soon it began to move toward me, then layers upon layers of rings of light moved, creating the feeling of flying through a tunnel. I felt the pain subside as my spirit lifted ever so slightly. I perceived the black things moving toward me all at once, but before they reached me, something else appeared.

I found myself suddenly surrounded by three entities, each made of pure light. One stood to the right of me. She appeared as a powerful, glowing being consisting of the most beautiful amber light, the same color as the astral world whenever I spirit-traveled. I could barely make out her features but noticed dark, loving eyes amid the beautiful, familiar, amber light. To my right stood another almost identical being, except her light shone as the purist white. Had I perceived it with my eyes, I felt it could have blinded me. In this place, just beyond the physical, the whiteness brought me great peace and comfort. The two beings had their arms stretched out tilted downward, with palms facing my body as if preparing to pick me up.

Above me I saw the most extraordinary being of all. She floated directly above my body, her calm, softly smiling face inches from my own. Her long hair moved gently as if underwater. She glowed with the deepest, most brilliant indigo I had ever seen.

Those three entities filled my soul and my body with their amazing light and energy. I felt it viscerally. I felt completely safe and filled with love and pure light. I vaguely wondered if they had come to escort me to the afterlife. When I felt them lift my spirit up a little further from my body, I thought that I had indeed died. They took me no further though, but simply gently cradled my spirit while my body burned a foot below my conscious self.

I do not know how long I lingered there with my three allies, as I came to call them, but at some point I opened my eyes, finding myself lying on my back, soaked, but not shivering. As I moved my eyes around the room I saw that the dark things had gone, and that I did not feel the same pain as I had hours before. I carefully turned my head expecting the splitting, throbbing pain to return, but it did not. Before long, Mom came in.

"Hey ..." she said, gently sitting on the edge of the bed. "Look who's back among the living."

She leaned down to feel my temperature with the back of her hand.

"Your fever's finally broken. Do you suppose you could sit up if I help you?"

I nodded weakly, then tried to lift myself into a sitting position. I couldn't. The illness had weakened me greatly.

"It's okay," Mom said, "You've been sick a long time. It's going to take time for you to get your strength back. Can I help you into the bathroom? We can wash your face and get you into fresh pajamas, and I can change these linens."

Though the intense part of my illness subsided, I never really got better. I sipped broth, ate Jello, then finally, some solid food, but I never lost the weakness that gradually became profound fatigue. I felt as if something had invaded every cell in my body, and had no intention of leaving.

When I finally returned to school, I could barely stay awake. I would drag myself out of bed and into my school uniform. I felt drowsy while trying to eat a bowl of cereal. Mom gave me coffee, but it didn't help. I forced my eyelids open, but fell asleep in nearly every class.

When I came home from school, I dropped my school books by the stairs and flopped on the couch, almost immediately falling asleep until dinner. Awakened for the meal, I barely ate, and felt a deep brain fog. I could not read, but fell asleep after only a page or two. I could not work on my Egyptian studies. I wanted to do nothing except sleep. I could hardly bear the effort it took to reach over and pick up a glass of water on the table. I continued only by sheer force of will.

Then one night I awoke screaming in terrible pain. It felt as if my knees, fingers, and hips were being crushed in a vice. I screamed for Mom, who came running. With tears streaming down my cheeks, I described the excruciating pain.

"Maybe it's growing pains." she said, sitting on the bed next to me. "No!" I cried. "This is *not* growing pains. Something is *really* wrong with me. Look at my knees."

Pulling the covers back, my mother saw my hot, terribly swollen knees. "Did you fall down or get hurt at school?" She asked, puzzled.

"NO!" I replied, "Something is really wrong!"

Mom got me some aspirin and then gently rubbed my hot, swollen knees with her cool hands. The next day she made an appointment with our pediatrician, who we almost never saw.

Doctor Duffy came in as I sat on the examining table, barely covered in a gown, with Mom sitting in a chair in the corner. He had thick white hair, a red face, and a white coat. He asked Mom to describe the problem.

"She has no energy. She falls asleep in class and at the dinner table. This is not normal for her. She's usually quite active. Now she's having pain in her knees at night." Mom explained.

Though at fourteen I could have answered his questions, he never addressed me and barely even looked at me.

"Hmmm," he said, putting his stethoscope in his ears. "Let's have a listen."

He never looked at my knees which bulged profusely between my thin thighs and calves. He turned to Mom, and with a smug smile said,

"I think I can diagnose this right now. It's called L-A-Z-Y."

My face flushed with embarrassment. I had already considered the possibility that I was a hypochondriac and had made it all up in my head. I felt my eyes begin to well up when Mom stood up and moved within inches of Doctor Duffy.

She looked him squarely in the eye with the face of a mother lion and said, "F-U-C-K! Y-O-U!"

Then she turned to me and said, "Get dressed. We are getting out of here." Then turning back to the good doctor, she said, "And we are not paying you a dime for this either! Go ahead and sue us. My husband is a lawyer!"

Doctor Duffy left the room, and we left the office amidst a flurry of disapproving nurses and receptionists.

When we got in the car, Mom said, "Asshole quack. Lazy, my ass!"

Then we drove out of the parking lot and home.

After that, we visited one doctor after another. I had multiple blood tests with no conclusions. I learned how to push through the fatigue and focus away from the pain in my body by lightly touching my face or arm until I felt nothing but the tickle, tricking my brain into ignoring the pain.

After a year of seeking a diagnosis, we found a highly respected orthopedic surgeon. He had saved my Aunt Marilyn's leg after it had been crushed in a terrible car accident. I liked him right away. He reminded me of Dr. Livingood, the Egyptian language professor at The University of Chicago who had helped me learn Hieroglyphics. He appeared rather unkempt, like a wacky scientist, but completely serious. He ordered another battery of tests that included x-rays, bloodwork, and more.

After many weeks, Mom and I went to his office for a consultation. He sat behind a big, cluttered desk, shuffling a small stack of reports and test results. He did not look at me, but spoke directly to Mom in a somber tone.

"Well," he said, "These tests seem to contradict each other in some ways, but we could chalk that up to normal abnormalities. Looking at these tests and the clinical data it seems that your daughter suffers from Juvenile Rheumatoid Arthritis."

My head shot up, and I could focus on nothing other than the words *Rheumatoid Arthritis.*

Grammie Ethel suffered from Rheumatoid Arthritis. It caused great pain and disability, and left her body ravaged and horribly disfigured. I felt terror and dread at the thought of that as my own fate.

Mom asked questions that I barely heard until he answered, "No cure. Unfortunately, it will continue to progress until she is completely crippled. Most children who suffer from JRA don't live through their thirties."

I sat in stunned silence. At fifteen, I received a death sentence. Worse, my slog to the grave would destroy my body in a most painful and disfiguring way. I stopped listening as Mom asked about treatments. Dr. Fahey said he had some experimental surgical treatments, but we could talk about that at another visit. Right now, we had a lot to soak in.

Mom thanked him. We walked to the car in complete silence with the words *Rheumatoid Arthritis* ringing in my brain. Sitting on the bench seat in the front of the big station wagon, Mom looked over at me and smiled.

"Let's go to The Buffalo."

I nodded in agreement even though it was not yet noon. The Buffalo was a well-known and spectacular ice cream parlor in our old neighborhood. They made their own ice cream and had a great variety of sundaes with names like Tutti Fruity or Big Buster.

We sat in a booth, and each ordered our own sundae. I remembered going there on hot summer nights when we lived in the old house, and all I had to worry about were the spirits. We would buy one big sundae, and all get a spoon to share it across the table.

"Extra whipped cream and cherries!" Mom called after the waitress.

Then she reached across the table and took my hands in hers, squeezing gently to not hurt my swollen knuckles.

"I know this is terrible news." she said, "It's just an awful thing." Her green eyes looked deeply into mine. "But we have to remember that the only thing different from yesterday is that now we have more information."

I nodded. *Information.* I liked information. I could deal with information.

"I'll be okay, Mom," I said.

"You'll be better than okay, "she replied. At last, we have a doctor who knows what he's doing." Then under her breath, she said, "Lazy," shook her head and let go of my hands as our ice cream arrived.

CHAPTER 6: TAUNT

[tönt] *transitive verb*, to challenge in a mocking manner.

As I BEGAN TREATMENT, I continued as I always had, going to school Monday through Friday and babysitting on weekends. My godmother, Patricia Ann, for whom I frequently babysat, had recommended me to a new family who had recently moved to an affluent neighborhood with many old and opulent homes several towns away from where I lived.

When Mr. Wright arrived to pick me up, he came inside to introduce himself to my family and to leave contact information, since we did not know him. Although he seemed friendly enough, I felt surprisingly nervous. He made small talk, asking questions about my interests and school during the twenty-minute drive to his home, and my post. I learned that he worked with Patricia Ann's husband as an attorney, and that he and his wife had one child, an eighteen-month-old boy whom he obviously adored. I began to relax, enjoying the easy conversation. Then we turned off the side street past the dim light posts at the end of his driveway.

The house loomed massive and foreboding before me. Darkened windows caught the reflection of the headlights as we approached the home where I would spend the evening babysitting. The only sign of life came from a small light above the front door on the porch. I noticed with some trepidation that no interior lights shone through the windows on the front of the house.

"This is it," said Mr. Wright, turning the key in the ignition of his newer model luxury car. "Home sweet home."

My anxiety escalated as I noticed the significant distance between the houses beyond their expansive yard. Mr. Wright opened my car door, and I stepped out into the cool night air. I looked up at all the darkened windows trying not to reveal my anxiety.

"C'mon in," he said, "I'll introduce you to the wife."

He flipped on a light in the front foyer. The moment I stepped over the threshold, I recognized that all-too-familiar, heart-dropping feeling of something else in that house. I swallowed hard as I followed him inside, closing the heavy door behind me.

My spirit senses tingled as I quickly glanced around. To my left I noticed a wide staircase that turned and disappeared around a broad landing. Beyond the staircase lay a beautifully decorated parlor lit only by the light from the foyer ceiling. We turned right and made our way through an enormous darkened formal dining room with a long table surrounded by chairs, sideboards, and tall china cabinets. The deep red rug and darkly stained wood seemed to absorb any light that fell in from the front entry. On the far end of the dining room we came to a heavy wooden swinging door that led to a short passage and into the lit kitchen.

"There's my beautiful bride." He kissed his wife affectionately on the cheek, "Meet our ace babysitter." Then, turning to me said, "This is Mrs. Wright."

Mrs. Wright wore a beautiful champagne-colored satin cocktail dress. Her high heels matched her dress perfectly. Glistening diamond earrings with a matching necklace accentuated her perfect blonde hair and meticulously made up face.

She smiled warmly as we shook hands.

"You are in for an easy night," she declared. "The baby is already asleep, and he *never* wakes once he's down."

Famous last words, I thought, still sensing the presence of something other than the Wrights in that house.

"Come with me, and I'll show you to the nursery."

I followed her through another door into a den lined with shelves of leather-bound books accentuated by elegant vases and classical statues. Though side lamps beside the sofa, and on a table between a pair of overstuffed chairs lit the room, the dark woodwork and area rug made it appear shrouded in shadow.

Mrs. Wright led me to a long narrow staircase behind a heavy wooden door at the far side of the den. She turned to me and put a finger to her lips.

"Shhh," she whispered, "The nursery is right up here."

A stab of panic pierced my chest as she began ascending the stairs. Mustering all my courage, I followed close behind. The staircase had no light of its own. The only light came from the room below and the light in the hall at the top of the stairs. Reaching out with my arms, I easily touched both walls without stretching. I felt claustrophobic and anxious, sensing that whomever, or whatever, shared the house with the Wright family lurked mere inches from my back as we climbed the stairs far too slowly. I wished that Mrs. Wright would move faster so I could escape that space. With each step, my anxiety escalated. When we finally reached the last step, I noticed another door at the top of the stairs.

Who builds a staircase with a door at each end, and no light of its own? I thought incredulously.

Mrs. Wright quietly opened a door to our right.

"Here's my little angel," She whispered. "You'll find diapers and a change of pajamas in the changing table if you need them ... which I'm sure you won't."

The baby lay sleeping peacefully in his crib with his bottom in the air, a colorful mobile dangled above him. I noticed a white rocking chair, dresser, and a shelf filled with stuffed toys. Mrs. Wright motioned for me to exit quietly. Once through the door she pulled it, leaving it slightly ajar.

"I'll just leave this open a little so you can hear him if he starts to stir." she whispered. "You should keep the stairwell doors open too so you can hear him."

Mrs. Wright headed back down the stairs. Before entering the staircase I paused momentarily noticing several closed doors lining a long hallway. I assumed that the stairway I had seen when I entered the house lay somewhere in the dark toward the end of it. The hair on my neck stood on end, and I shuddered. Then, as quickly as my legs would allow, I followed her back to the main floor.

Instructing me to help myself, Mrs. Wright showed me where to find snacks and soda in the kitchen, then she wrote a number where I could reach them in case of an emergency, and placed it next to the phone.

"Make yourself at home," she said, slipping her arms into the sleeves of the coat her husband held for her. "We should be back close to midnight."

After hearing the front door close and lock, and the car driving off, I returned to the den. I thought that watching TV might serve to thwart the extremely uncomfortable feeling I had that something loomed nearby. Unfortunately I discovered no TV in the den. I didn't even find a radio there or in the kitchen to fill the charged atmosphere with sound. *Everybody* had a TV by 1970. I wondered if they had a separate TV room in that expansive house. Recalling the uneasy feeling I had upon arrival, and the fact that the only lights burning in the house were in the kitchen, den, and the hallway upstairs I decided against a search. Instead I found a bottle of Coke® in the refrigerator, opened it, then settled on the most comfortable-looking couch in the den, and pulled out my books.

The silence grew increasingly distracting. I rarely, if ever, experienced silence in my world. It was easier to concentrate in the midst of my noisy family than in this dark, ominous, old house, so I began to hum.

BANG!

I jumped to my feet with tears stinging my eyes and my heart racing.

"What was that?!" I said aloud to nobody.

I stood frozen, listening for the sound of the baby, certain that such an abrupt sound surely must've woken him. I heard nothing. My sense of responsibility propelled me to investigate the source of the bang.

It sounded as though it came from upstairs. I set my books on the couch and gingerly made my way to the bottom of the stairs. Looking up, I discovered that the door at the top of the stairs had slammed closed. My heart dropped. I stood with my hand covering my mouth for several minutes, debating whether I should climb those stairs to open the door and check on the baby ... or not.

At last, I took a deep breath, fixed my eyes on the sliver of light shining through the crack at the bottom of the door, and made my way up as quickly as my damaged legs could carry me. I tried to push the horrific thought of becoming trapped in that stairwell to the back of my mind, though I could not ignore the terrible flutter in my gut and the hair raised on my neck and arms. I began to question if the door would even open in my hand when I reached it, or if I was entering a trap.

To my great relief, I made it to the top of the stairs safely. The door opened easily without even a squeak. I pushed it all the way open against the wall, and crept into the nursery.

Opening the door, I saw the baby, clearly undisturbed by the sound. I looked around the darkened room, making sure everything remained in its place. Moving silently to the crib, I placed my hand just above his tiny back to feel his warmth, and take note of his steady breathing.

Part of me felt relieved that he did not wake up, and yet another part wished he had so I would have some human company, and something to do other than stress about slamming doors, or the growing reality that something unseen wanted to get my attention. Remembering my mother's wise counsel to never wake a sleeping baby, I turned from the crib and quietly exited the nursery.

With senses piqued, I closed the nursery door, leaving it open a few inches, then turned toward the long, upstairs hallway. My stomach lurched as I took in every closed door that lined it. I felt a strong sensation that somebody lurked behind one of those doors. I listened acutely for any sound or movement concealed behind them, wondering if, perhaps, someone else remained in the house with me. My mind raced with thoughts of a creepy grandpa or uncle hidden in one of those rooms.

I quickly dispatched that thought, realizing that Mr. and Mrs. Wright certainly would have told me if someone else lived there with them.

Turning toward the stairwell I gasped, grabbing the door frame as my knees buckled. The door at the bottom of the stairs was now closed tightly! I had not heard it close. I had made sure it was fully open before I came upstairs. The thought of reentering that stairwell with doors that closed on their own at the top and bottom made me feel nauseous. I looked anxiously down the hall, and back toward the nursery trying to figure out the best way to proceed.

I needed a way to secure the upstairs door so that it could not possibly close while I was in the stairwell, or after I returned to the first floor. Noticing a long wool hall runner, I decided to use it to prop the door open. Grabbing the edge with both hands, I struggled to pull the heavy rug toward the stairwell door. I folded over the end, creating a barrier beyond which the door could not possibly swing on its own. Feeling confident that the door would not slam shut, I made my way back down the stairs.

Walking downstairs on my arthritic legs posed a greater difficulty for me than walking up. Each step sent pain shooting through my knees.

I prayed that the downstairs door would open without incident when I reached it. It did.

Relieved, I returned to my books on the couch. My hands trembled as I picked up my workbook and pencil to return to my studies. I rationalized the doors closing by telling myself that maybe someone hung them wrong, or that perhaps the old floor was uneven, causing gravity to allow the doors to swing shut on their own. I took a deep breath and focused upon the pages of my book. The silence grew more overwhelming and oppressive. I found it impossible to concentrate. Finishing my Coke, I made my way to the kitchen to deposit the empty bottle and grab a second Coke and a snack. Looking at the kitchen clock, I realized that I had been there just over an hour. I had nearly three more hours to endure. The *pop* and *hiss* from the Coke bottle as I opened it brought welcome relief from the silence. I grabbed a bag of potato chips and pulled it open with a deliberately boisterous rustle. Leaning against the counter, I took a few chips from the bag, and put them in my mouth, allowing the crunch to fill my ears. Then I took a long swig of the fizzy pop, following it up with an audible, *ahhh*, that ended in a long surprising *burp*.

Chuckling to myself, I made my way back to the den with chips and pop in hand. Freezing in my tracks as I entered the room, I nearly dropped both when I saw the stairwell door—once again closed.

This is ridiculous! I thought. *This is just insane!*

I knew I had to open the door. I also now began to realize that something did this intentionally. Something unseen taunted me. I wanted to call Mom, but what would I say? What could she do? What could I do? Nothing. Nothing at all.

Looking around the room, I noticed a heavy wooden chair. I set my chips and coke on the coffee table, and dragged the chair over to the stairwell door. Dread pierced my senses as I turned the door handle. Too frightened for what I might see behind the door, I looked away, quickly swinging it open. To my relief, when I turned back toward the stairs, I saw nothing otherworldly or frightening. I pushed the door against the wall and secured the sturdy chair in front of it. Standing at the bottom of the stairs, looking up to the brightly lit hallway upstairs, I listened for the sound of the baby but heard only silence once more.

Fully shaken, I returned to the couch. I kept my eyes trained on the open door as I put the coke bottle to my lips and drank. I tried to think of something else, knowing that I had secured each door in place. My focus remained fixed on the stairwell and the tiny sleeping child at the top of it. I began to whisper familiar prayers.

> *Hail Mary, full of grace, the Lord is with thee.*
> *Blessed art thou amongst women,*
> *And blessed is the fruit of thy womb, Jesus.*
> *Holy Mary, Mother of God, pray for us sinners,*
> *Now, and at the hour of our death....*

No! I thought, *Not that one. I don't want to think about the hour of anybody's death right now.*

That thought made me laugh. I needed to stop working myself up. I had to ignore my vivid imagination and focus on my babysitting job.

"This is just a big, dark, creepy house. I'm making this all up." I said to the open door and the empty room.

"*BANG!*"

Jumping to my feet I felt my heart leap in my chest.

"Holy Mary. Holy Mary. Holy Mary" I repeated as I cautiously crossed the room toward the stairwell, dreading what I might find.

"No, no, no, no, no," I said, shaking my head. "No, no, no. This is not happening."

The upstairs door was shut! I wanted to run. I wanted to just leave the door closed. The baby had not stirred despite everything that had transpired so far that evening. Mrs. Wright said he never woke up once down. Maybe I could just leave it be, but she had specifically instructed me to keep the doors open.

Then I heard him. Small whimpers came from behind the closed door above. I rubbed my face frantically with my open hands, listening, hoping that he would settle down without me. Then I began to wonder whether whatever taunted me had disturbed the helpless baby as well. I contemplated the real possibility that something unseen was using the baby to lure me back into the stairwell. Though it terrified me, my protective sense outweighed my fear. Jostling the chair blocking the downstairs door to make sure it held fast, I mustered every ounce of courage and began climbing the stairs toward the closed door at the top, listening to the muffled sounds of a stirring baby behind it.

Any comfort from attributing the evening's disturbances to my vivid imagination dissolved in terror as I opened the door to find the heavy hall runner back in its original place down the hallway. I clenched my teeth, pursed my lips, and steeled my resolve. My breath came short and fast as I entered the nursery, leaving the door open behind me to allow the hall light to fill the room.

The baby stirred in his sleep. I leaned over the edge of the crib and placed a firm but gentle hand on his back, humming a repetitive tune soft and low. Feeling his little warm body gave me some comfort. I was not alone. I had this tiny sleeping person there with me ... my charge ... my responsibility.

Before long, he settled back down breathing peacefully. From the crib I could see that the stairwell door remained open. I gently lifted my hand from the baby's back and tiptoed out the door, closing it behind me. I hated this place. I wanted to leave and sit out on the front steps until Mr. and Mrs. Wright returned. I did not want to stay another minute.

"Hello," I called softly down the hall.

I looked down at the rug, then up at the many closed doors down the hall, with shadows growing deeper the further down I looked. "Hello," I repeated, but nothing answered.

Then I turned toward the stairwell door and made my way to the top of the stairs.

My whole body shook, and I nearly burst into tears when I saw that, once again, the door at the bottom of the stairs was closed. Gravity could not have moved the heavy chair I placed to prop it open. Something lurked in this dark place, and that something had its sights set on me. My terror turned to tenacity. I needed to protect both myself and that helpless little baby in the room behind me. Done playing, I returned to the nursery.

Leaning over the sleeping child, I whispered, "I've got this. Nothing will come in here tonight."

Moving the rocking chair to the center of the room and facing it squarely toward the door, I sat down and began to rock deliberately and rhythmically back and forth. I focused on the energy contained just under my skin. With each rock forward, I exhaled, pushing my energy from the place just above my navel out toward the nursery door. As I rocked back, I calmly inhaled, making sure that I did not draw my energy back inside myself. After several minutes focusing on my breath, I created a large balloon made of my own protective energy designed to hold anything that dared attempt to enter at bay. I called on my guardian angel to stand guard with me.

I held that energy in place for hours until I heard footsteps down-stairs. Sitting at attention, I listened to the sound of the stairwell door opening. Holding my breath, I listened acutely, ready for whatever came next.

"Hello?" Mrs. Wright called softly as she climbed the stairs.

My back and neck ached as I finally exhaled, releasing the energy barrier I had held for so long.

I met her at the top of the stairs.

"Is everything okay?" she whispered.

I nodded motioning for us to go downstairs.

"The doors wouldn't stay open," I told her. "Both doors kept closing even after I blocked them with a chair or the rug upstairs. Does that happen?"

Mrs. Wright looked puzzled, "I don't know." she said flatly.

"Well," I went on, "I couldn't keep them open, and I wasn't sure I would hear the baby if he woke up, so I decided to just spend the evening in the rocking chair in his room."

"You are such a dear." she smiled, "Now I see why Patricia Ann told me you were the best babysitter ever. Thank you."

I wanted to tell her about my terrifying ordeal and ask her if she knew that her house was haunted. Mostly I just wanted to leave, so I simply smiled sheepishly and thanked her. She opened her pocketbook and took out a twenty dollar bill. I charged seventy-five cents an hour. I did not reach for the bill. No one had ever paid that much for any babysitting job.

Seeing my shock, she said, "Here. Take it, you earned it. Thank you so much."

Mrs. Wright walked me through the dark house to the front door where I saw Mr. Wright waiting in the warm car to take me home.

She waved as I got in, saying, "Thank you, I'll call you again."

My body felt stiff with exhaustion from exerting such massive amounts of protective energy for so long in that perilous house.

"How'd it go?" asked Mr. Wright, swinging onto the main street.

I turned to look at him. His face glowed in the dim light of the dashboard as he put on his blinker and slowed for a red light. Stopping, he faced me, smiling.

"Do the doors in your house close on their own?" I asked.

"What? What do you mean?"

"The doors, the stairwell doors, do they close on their own?"

The light turned green. Mr. Wright focused back on the road.

"I don't think so. I haven't noticed anything. Why? Did you have trouble with the doors?"

"Nevermind," I said, facing the side window to watch the trees and houses fly by.

Reaching home at last, he asked if his wife had paid me.

"Yes, very well, thank you."

Before closing the car door I leaned down and said, "You know, you should check them." He looked puzzled. "The doors, I mean. Maybe the hinges are loose or something."

"Goodnight," He said, confused.

"Goodnight," I replied, then hurried up the walk to my own front door, relieved beyond measure for the end of my ordeal and my own peaceful house.

When Mrs. Wright called the next week, I told her I already had a job, which was true, but the next time she called, I told her that I had booked a regular babysitting job every weekend. I gave her the name of a couple of my older sister's friends from school who lived closer to the Wrights and who also babysat.

Hanging up, I hoped those other girls might not notice the other-worldly energy that inhabited that frightening house and enjoy an *easy* babysitting job. I, however, had no intention of setting foot in that place ever again for the rest of my life.

Chapter 7: Leering

[Lir-iŋ] *verb*, a lascivious, knowing, or wanton look

My best friend Jenny and I giggled as we made our way up the long open wooden stairs to the costume room in the ancient theater. Other cast and crew members busied themselves in various parts of the building that stood on the expansive grounds of the Divine Word Seminary.

Built in 1899, it first served the Brothers of the Divine Word as a technical school where they housed and educated orphan boys, then later to train young men to become Christian Brothers who would serve as missionaries around the world.

The theater, located some distance away from the main building, had suffered from many years of neglect when our community theater group discovered and leased it. We cleaned, scrubbed, and repainted. We replaced the stage lights and updated the facility to meet the needs of a blossoming community theater company.

The theater had three levels, including the main performance space that consisted of a large stage complete with catwalks, rigging, curtains, and multiple backdrops. It had a large workroom and storage room in the back, plus nearly a dozen dressing rooms lining a long, narrow hallway off stage right, along with an equal number in the basement. It also had an upstairs costume room overflowing with wardrobes filled with seemingly endless treasures hidden away after long-ago performances from Shakespeare to Gilbert and Sullivan.

I joined the theater group before my freshman year in high school.

I loved singing and dancing in the chorus. We put on musicals such as *Brigadoon, Carousel,* and *Mame.* Jenny and I went to different schools. She was a year younger than me, but we both shared a wild, unconventional, and joyful approach to life. Whenever we spent time together, we would find fun and sometimes crazy things to do.

On one work day at the theater, Jenny and I volunteered to organize the costume room. Going through hundreds of ancient costumes and props seemed like the most epic dress-up game of all time! We needed to purge anything that had rotted beyond use, then take inventory of what we had left that we could use in future productions.

While everyplace in the theater seemed full of otherworldly energy, the costume room located far away from everything else felt especially charged. Dust particles swirled and floated in the musty air illuminated by streams of sunlight pouring through tall windows against the back wall.

"This is going to be a blast!" Jenny exclaimed, stepping out of her jeans.

I closed the door as she stripped off her shirt and dropped it on her jeans. She flashed me a conspiratorial grin and headed for the nearest wardrobe.

Feeling self-conscious about my pubescent body and bulging, swollen joints, I hesitated as Jenny pulled out a long, medieval-looking, dusty rose, velveteen dress with a golden cable sash.

"Hurry up! This will look really groovy on you."

She shoved the dress toward me, flashing her bright, inviting smile. I took a deep breath and stripped down to my underwear, then quickly grabbed the dress from her hands and slipped it over my head.

"Here, let me help you," she said, reaching for the cable sash to tie behind my back.

"Let's have a look!" She grabbed both my shoulders, turned me around to face her, and took a couple of steps backward.

I felt embarrassed as she sized me up and down while standing there in her underwear. Then she approached me and grabbed the ample fabric that should have been filled by a bust in both hands.

"Looks good," she said, "We can just stuff some toilet paper or socks in here, and it will be perfect!"

My face turned crimson as she laughed uproariously, bending over to slap her knees.

"Nice," I said, turning to the wardrobe, "Let's find something for you."

We doubled over in laughter when I pulled a rotting, purple and gold jester's costume from the cupboard and thrust it toward her.

"This has your name all over it," I laughed.

Just then, we heard footsteps on the rickety wooden stairs. Jenny dramatically thrust her arm across her chest and spread her hand to cover the front of her underpants, with her knees together and her feet apart. She attempted to stifle an uncontrollable giggle.

"Shhhh," I said to Jenny, then moved toward the closed door. "We are in here. Who's there?"

Nobody answered.

"Hello?" I repeated with my face inches from the door.

Jenny could not stop giggling, "I have to pee." she laughed.

I turned back to her and put a finger to my lips.

"Maybe we are being too loud," I whispered, "Hello?"

I slowly turned the door handle and pulled it open a few inches so I could peek out. Nobody was on the stairs. I stepped out on the small landing in front of the door and looked to the space below, expecting to see someone on the stage, or slipping away to avoid detection, but I saw nobody at all. Suddenly Jenny, still in her underwear, sidled up behind me to have a look for herself.

"Must've been something else," she said, turning back to the wardrobe.

But the air seemed to have drained from the room. A chill ran down my spine, and I had the unmistakable sense that someone watched us.

"Who's up here?" I called out, turning to assess the entire room.

"Do you feel that?" I asked Jenny.

"What?" she asked.

Just then the footsteps on the stairs resumed. We could not deny that they came closer and closer to the door. I sensed a dangerous presence with terrible intentions approaching.

"Get dressed." I commanded Jenny. "Put something on."

I felt someone watching us with lustful intent.

"Whoever is there, go away!" I commanded, but the steps continued until I knew he was just outside the door.

Jenny grew bold. "Hey you creep! Go away and stop spying on naked teenagers!" Then she started to giggle nervously into her hands.

Quickly, I swung the door open, expecting to catch one of the creepy guys from the company spying on us, but again saw nothing.

"This isn't fun anymore," said Jenny pulling her jeans over her hips, "This is too creepy. Let's get outta here."

I quickly removed the costume and dressed in my own clothes. We hung the dress back in the wardrobe, and skedaddled out of there as fast as we could.

CHAPTER 8: MORPH

[mȯrf] *transitive verb*, to undergo transformation
from an image of one object into that of another

AFTER BECOMING ILL, I COULD NO LONGER DANCE in the theater company,
but I could sing and do bit parts. When I had my first surgery, however,
I could not participate on stage at all because I had to use crutches or a
wheelchair. Eventually, I found my niche painting backdrops, doing stage
makeup, and even assisting the director. I loved the theater, every aspect
of it.

One spring Saturday, Jenny and I consented to paint heavy canvas
backdrops for our upcoming production on the stage. Lit only by the work
lights above, we gleefully painted away in the dark and musty theater.

Though a bright, perfect spring day bloomed outside, neither of us
minded in the least. We loved participating in community theater. We
loved how the adults in the group valued and honored our artistic and
theatrical gifts. It felt wonderful to participate in something beyond the
petty cruelty and judgement so often demonstrated by our peers and
teachers at school.

Hearing the sound of someone entering through the doors in the
back of the theater, Jenny and I looked up simultaneously. We expected
to see one of our fellow crew members arriving to help out. Instead we
saw an empty theater. Squinting, I looked closely to make sure the darkened back of the theater hadn't obscured whomever we heard enter. We
looked at each other puzzled and confused.

"You heard somebody come in, right?" Jenny asked.

I nodded and shrugged. We turned and got back to work painting in uneasy silence when we heard a loud, distinct THUMP from the back of the theater. It sounded as if somebody slammed an open hand on the wooden back of one of the theater seats. Startled, we jumped and quickly swung around. The hair on my arms stood on end, and an icy chill filled the room. We sat transfixed as we watched a tall, ethereal figure begin to glide down the center aisle toward us. He tucked his hands inside the sleeves of a long hooded robe. He didn't walk but appeared to float. Jenny pulled me to my feet as he slid closer. We grabbed each other's hands. Not waiting for him to reach the stage or us, we ran squealing and laughing hysterically off the stage. Jenny raced through the wings, while I limped as fast as possible toward the dressing rooms where we hoped to find adults.

"What the heck is going on with you two?" The director exclaimed as we bolted toward her.

"We saw a ghost! We saw a ghost of a monk in the theater coming towards us!!!" We both stammered breathlessly.

"Oh, for crying out loud!" She said, "You two need to stop messing around, or we will never stay on schedule," she said, shaking her head and telling us to get back to work and to save the drama for the play.

We refused.

"No way are we going back there alone!" said Jenny. "That monk did not look friendly!"

"Fine," she said with exasperation, "You two can help sweep out these dressing rooms. There's fifty years of dust in here."

Relieved, we agreed. Jenny picked up a pail of soapy water, I scooped up a pile of rags, and walked down the long narrow row of dressing rooms, giggling nervously. Halfway down, we found the first unopened room. Glancing at Jenny and still shaken by our experience on the stage, I turned the porcelain door handle and cautiously pushed the door open. A blast of frigid air stopped us in our tracks. We stood in the doorway, immediately sensing that we were not alone. Before I had time to turn on the ancient, rotating light switch, we noticed a bluish glow in the opposite corner of the small room. The nebulous apparition began to materialize into the very figure we had seen in the theater moments before! It had followed us!

Screaming and laughing uncontrollably, we dropped the pail, raced from the room, and flew down the hallway toward the emergency exit. We burst through the door into bright, blinding sunlight. Jenny kept running away from the theater, still laughing and screaming. I moved as quickly as my disabled body would allow, but the distance between us quickly grew.

"C'mon! Catch up!" She shouted from further and further away, "Let's check out the grotto!"

Unable to take another step, I needed rest to regain both strength and composure. I stopped in front of a tall, white stone statue of a mysterious female saint. No marker revealed her identity. I stood beneath and looked up into her face.

Suddenly a strong gust of wind made my long hair fly in front of my face, obscuring my vision. I pushed it back behind my ears repeatedly, only to have the maelstrom continue to blow in my eyes. As this happened, I began to notice subtle changes in the face of the statue. It appeared to morph into various faces at an ever increasing speed. I held my hair with both hands to see more clearly as one after another female face appeared on the statue.

Something continued to block my view as if unseen fingers flashed in my field of vision. I realized it could not be my hair, though it felt like hair, or perhaps spider webs. Though I had no clue what or who, something or someone kept me from seeing clearly. The faces became illuminated as they changed over and over again until it appeared as if a thousand women's faces flashed before my eyes. At last, both the wind and the morphing ceased abruptly. I stood alone in the glaring sunshine, gazing into the stone face of a mysterious woman. Maybe from her, or from someplace inside my head, or perhaps even the depths of the universe itself, I heard a low-pitched androgynous voice declare:

"There will be three."

"Three what?" I asked aloud.

Suddenly I heard Jenny calling me from the grotto in the distance. I turned and began to make my way toward her, feeling light-headed and confused but also euphoric in an odd way. When I reached the grotto, I descended the few stone stairs out of the bright afternoon sun and into the dim dankness of the subterranean grotto.

A monk had built the grotto in the early days of the seminary, digging into the ground and placing every rock by hand. It contained a life-sized statue of Christ in the garden of Gethsemane. The paint on its hands and face had cracked and chipped in many places. The faded colors of the robe were quite lifelike. The statue knelt with his hands clasped in prayer, his tormented face tilted toward light from an opening in the stone roof above. Dusty, faded, plastic flowers and greenery surrounded him. A three-foot stone wall separated the diorama from the viewing area, where I found Jenny staring pensively at the statue of Jesus. She turned to me and smiled broadly.

"This place is really creepy." She said

"This place? The grotto?" I asked.

"No, this whole place. Mostly the theater ..." She turned back to gaze at the diorama.

I tried to explain my experience with the changing statue when she grabbed my hand. I noticed an extremely alarmed expression on her face.

"Look!" She whispered, gesturing with her head while not breaking her intense stare, "What's happening to the statue?"

"What?" I turned to look at the statue of Christ. I noticed smooth colors in the garments where paint had moments before appeared flaked and cracked. I looked more closely and saw the painted hair soften and flow—moving with the airflow. I looked at its face, and saw the eyes close and open. I noticed its neck flex as if swallowing.

"Oh my god!" I whispered, "Are you seeing this?"

Jenny put her hands to her mouth. Her eyes filled with terror and tears as she slowly nodded.

"STOP IT!" I shouted, "STOP IT NOW!"

I did not know who or what had inhabited the statue of Christ in the Garden of Gethsemane, but whom or whatever began to turn its gaze towards us. I stood my ground fiercely as it caught my eyes and stared threateningly into the very depths of my soul.

"Get back:" I shouted.

The stone figure began to rise as if attempting to move closer to us. Jenny whimpered.

"Take my hand!" I told her urgently, never breaking eye contact with the statue. "We need to do this together."

Raising our clasped hands and facing our free palms toward the animated statue, we shouted, "NO! Get back! Go away!"

A surge of energy I had never felt before came from somewhere outside of me, bolted into my body, and flew like a charged golden light through my solar plexus and outstretched hands. Instantly, the once-terrifying being returned to plaster and faded, peeling paint. Jenny turned to me, aghast and shaking.

"We've got to get out of here!" She cried, turning to flee from the grotto.

I stood there for another moment or two, trying to make sense of the crazy events of the day—trying to figure out if *what I knew happened* actually did happen. Then I heard Jenny calling me from outside.

"Look! Quick! Oh my gosh! Hurry!"

Thinking perhaps another threat awaited, I quickly exited the dank grotto. My eyes needed time to adjust to the intense sunlight, so I rubbed them as Jenny continued to shout my name from further and further away. When I could finally see, I saw her in a distant field. Also, in the far-off field, a beautiful, pure white horse ran with Jenny following behind, laughing and squealing with delight.

"Look! A horse escaped the barns!" She laughed, "C'mon! Let's catch it!"

A wave of sorrow and loneliness washed over me. My thumbs and throat throbbed and ached. I watched Jenny run freely after that gorgeous white horse, knowing somehow that she would not be with me for much longer. I could not run. I could not keep up. I knew that I would need to figure out my life ahead alone. I knew that my broken body would take me on a completely different journey than my dear friend Jenny, whom I loved. My heart broke. I turned away from her and walked a different path that led to a series of small shrines depicting The Stations of the Cross.

Weeds choked the earth near the shrines, infiltrating the gravel pathway. As a Catholic schoolgirl, I knew the Way of the Cross by heart, and though the engraved inscriptions were weathered and mostly illegible, I recited the devotions in my head as I walked along in the warm sunshine. Each shrine consisted of a pedestal of field rocks embedded in rough concrete. The top of each encased a small, realistic plaster sculpture inside an arched stone diorama.

At last, I came to the thirteenth station. It contained a miniature replica of Michelangelo's masterful sculpture, *The Pietà*, one of my most beloved works of art. I did not recall the prayer for this station. Growing up, I had only memorized the stations up to the crucifixion. The scene I now stood before depicted a scene after, when the Madonna cradled the body of her crucified son.

I felt the grief so elegantly carved in the face of the mother. It spoke to my own grief over the realization that my path ahead would not include loved ones, would not mirror the path of my peers, but would challenge me both physically and spiritually. Tears welled up as I tried to decipher the words carved in the pedestal. I gently rubbed my fingertips over the faded letters. Licking my fingers, I traced the weather-worn words. The moisture slowly revealed them.

"Great ... As ... The ... Sea ... Is ... My ... Sorrow." laboriously emerged from the lichen and cement.

My breath caught in my throat with an audible sob at the revelation of the final word. Tears rolled down my cheeks. As the moisture evaporated, obscuring the words, their gravity gripped my soul. I pitied myself and the life that I would have to endure. *"Great as the sea is my sorrow!"*

I shook my head sadly and returned my focus from the words to the beautiful sculpture. Blinking hard to clear my eyes of tears, I watched, stunned, as the very same menacing face from the grotto began to replace the face of Christ.

Feeling more rage than fear, I growled, "Get away from me! How dare you usurp something so beautiful! YOU HAVE NO POWER HERE!"

All on my own for the first time in my life, I mustered a power that came through me from the entirety of the universe and forcefully cast the intruder away.

The air seemed to grow lighter as I heard words resonate from all around me in the same voice that spoke to me at the statue of the woman:

"Great as the sea is my sorrow ... but no longer for thou art clean and alive and reflect all I know!"

My self-pity dissolved, and I grew euphoric and light-headed. I did not know what the voice meant. I did not know what any of the events of the day meant. I felt that I had stood some manner of trial and discovered a powerful connection to something magnificent and good far beyond my small, frail self.

Turning around, I watched Jenny laughing in the distant field as she continued to chase the mysterious white horse, the two of them running wild and free. I smiled with nothing but pure love in my heart. It no longer made me sad to think about her going on without me. I knew that though my path might take me on an unexpected journey in this life, I would always have constant and powerful allies. I believed they would remain with me forever, that had, perhaps, followed me through many lifetimes. I was "clean and alive." I did not yet know what I reflected, but I trusted it would become clearer in time.

Many years later, as I shared this story with my daughter, she asked if that date had any particular significance. I remembered that it happened on the first Saturday in May in my sixteenth year. She checked the calendar on her phone and found that the first Saturday in May in 1971 was the first day of May. Beltane.

CHAPTER 9: INVOKE

[in-'vōk] *transitive verb*, to call forth by incantation; conjure

ON ONE OF OUR LAST VISITS TO THE UNIVERSITY OF CHICAGO before Professor Livingood went to Ur on an excavation that would last the rest of her life, she gifted me a copy of a new graduate-level text and workbook. It contained multiple lessons on translating and transliterating *The Egyptian Book Of The Dead*. It proved an arduous task that required many steps to complete, even a single page. Nonetheless, I dove in wholeheartedly and, page by page, began working my way through my latest assignment.

The Egyptian Book Of The Dead was designed as a travel guide for the newly dead as they navigated the underworld toward everlasting life. It contains many incantations, directions, and descriptions of those one will meet and what to expect on one's journey to eternity.

I found it fascinating. I translated passages describing how Thoth would weigh the deceased's heart in a balance. If the heart was heavier than a feather, a terrible three-headed dog would devour the *ka* or soul of the dead. I enjoyed the knowledge that even these ancient people valued lightheartedness and goodness in life.

I loved translating who had to pay what to whom along the way in the elaborate text and relished the idea that the afterlife was as real a place as the world of the living for the ancient Egyptians. I often contemplated how humans have somehow always known that there is something beyond the physical world. Though the cosmology and mythology of ancient Egypt differed vastly from that of the modern world, I recognized similarities in the mythology. From the risen god, Osiris, to the trinity of Isis, Osiris, and Horus, humans have used stories to explain the unseen. I had experienced the unseen throughout my young life. I craved to learn how human beings interpreted the things I had experienced, so I immersed myself in the text that grew more familiar the deeper I went.

Before long, I translated long passages with increasing fluidity. Though mostly I had to labor through multiple steps, I sometimes found myself writing translations directly from the hieroglyphs, bypassing other phases.

After working my way through several sections, I began translating pages containing an invocation for Anubis, the chief Egyptian god of the underworld. One night I chose to work on the translations while waiting in the green room at the theater before a play in which I had a small part. I found that focusing on my hieroglyphics provided a perfect way for me to eliminate any pre-performance jitters. Sitting alone at a long table, I began to work.

I finished the first two lines of the text, carefully printing the translation in the space provided in my workbook. This was a multi-step process. I needed to transcribe both graphemes and pictographs *and then* transliterate each phrase. It required me to shift back and forth between the workbook and the text.

As I examined the hieroglyphs, I began to hear the ancient words in my head. Ancient Egyptian, as depicted in the hieroglyphics from the 18th Dynasty, is a dead language. Though linguists approximate how the spoken language might have sounded based on more recent languages of the region, there is no way to determine exactly how it actually sounded, and yet I heard it ... clearly ... resounding in my head.

Once again, my "vivid imagination" took over, and I heard the spoken words as I worked on the translation, not in English but in the dead language of four thousand years ago. At this point, I entered some kind of mental *zone* and began to lose my sense of the present and my immediate surroundings. After several minutes (I didn't know exactly how long), I returned to the moment, and looked down at my text and workbook. The text page remained on the last line I recalled consciously translating, but the workbook page no longer matched up. I had written three pages without knowing it. I had completed the invocation of Anubis in its entirety, while speaking it in my head, and perhaps, as far as I knew, aloud.

As I shook myself into full awareness, I noticed others in the green room doing their own thing. I quickly began where I had left off before my unconscious writing, carefully checking every phrase. My automatic, unconscious translation matched the text exactly.

All at once, I felt a foreboding presence very nearby. Again I looked around to the other actors who seemed to notice no change at all. The room grew icy cold, and I began to hear the words of the invocation again in my head in the ancient language. This terrified me. I felt as if something had tricked me into invoking an ancient god. It no longer felt like studying a dead language, but rather a recollection of things I, or someone who once was me, had done thousands of years prior. I had called in a dangerous and powerful entity that may have waited for me to remember how to speak its name to show itself.

I quickly pushed it out of my head and slammed both the text and the workbook shut, closing the connection that grew as I got closer to awakening that language in my own ancient memory.

It absolutely terrified me that this might actually exist in some other place, time, or dimension. I knew I could not control it but thought it could very likely control and even use me. I wanted nothing to do with this. I had not yet learned how to distinguish darkness from light. I did not yet understand that I could maintain my own power in the face of interdimensional power.

Closing the book ended my studies of Hieroglyphs, and I did not open it again for many years. Still, I never wholly closed the gate to that place and time. It continued to return in my dreams with ever-increasing clarity, and continues to this day.

CHAPTER 10: ENDURANCE

[in-'dûr-ən(t)s] *noun*, the ability to withstand hardship or adversity.

I BEGAN TO REGAIN CONSCIOUSNESS IN THE RECOVERY ROOM at Saint Francis Hospital in early March of 1971. I was sixteen years old. My body shivered violently, and nausea came in powerful waves. I heard the sound of moaning somewhere nearby and felt confused about its origin. As my brain grew clearer, I realized that the sound came from my own voice. My throat stung, and my mouth felt painfully parched. A blood pressure cuff tethered my right arm, and my left was strapped to a board to keep an IV line stable in my hand. My scalp tingled, and a strange antiseptic odor filled my nostrils, making my nose itch terribly. With both arms restricted, I could not reach up to relieve the itch, so I closed my eyes attempting to focus away from the discomfort, and to tap my fingertips together to trick my brain to ignore the itch. I had figured out this strategy in response to pain that I had no way of alleviating. I simply distracted my brain away from it.

"Oh no, you don't, Sleeping Beauty." A boisterous voice startled my eyes back open. "It's time to wake up. No going back to sleep now."

The recovery room nurse leaned in jostling me and began to pump up the blood pressure cuff until it grew painfully tight. I winced.

"It's okay, honey," she said, releasing the pressure and listening through her stethoscope.

She lifted a metal clipboard and wrote her findings down, then took other vital signs.

"How are you feeling? Would you like some ice chips?"
I tried to speak, but my dry and painful throat refused to cooperate,
so I nodded. She spooned a few ice chips into my mouth. I nodded,
attempted a smile, and asked for more. At the third spoonful, I began to
wretch.

She quickly turned my head to the side, shoving a stainless steel
tray under my chin with practiced expertise.

"Oh, dear. Let's just slow down here," she said. "You'll feel better
soon."

Again I closed my eyes. I just wanted to sleep. Suddenly my nausea
became overshadowed by an enormous pressure on my right leg. Again I
winced. It felt as if a heavy rock lay on top of my leg, crushing it entirely,
but mostly my knee.

"Ow, ow, ow," I whispered involuntarily, squeezing my eyes tightly.
"Open your eyes," she ordered, "It's time to start waking up."

"I am awake," I whispered hoarsely. "I just need to focus. I need to
make it stop hurting."

"We will get you something for that as soon as you are fully awake,"
she said, rubbing my cheek roughly with a gloved hand. "C'mon, honey.
Your mom is waiting for you in your room. We don't want to keep her
waiting all day, do we."

My room? Mom ... waiting? All day? What's going on? I felt so confused
... and cold .... Freezing cold. Again, my whole body began to shiver
violently, making my teeth chatter and increasing the pressure and pain
in my leg.

Suddenly I became aware of the nurse tucking warm flannel sheets
around my body. She tucked them under my chin and gently nudged
them tightly along my arms, side, and legs. Having learned my lesson
about closing my eyes, I forced myself to keep them open as I recalled
the old flannel receiving blankets we had at home. A tiny hint of a smile
crossed my face as I remembered Mom pulling them from the laundry
basket, still warm from the dryer, and wrapping them around me as I sat
on the couch barely awake in pain and fatigued by my mysterious illness.

I felt warm tears fall from the outside corners of my eyes and wished myself home.

"Oh dear," said the nurse, "I can see that you're in a lot of pain. You're awake enough now."

She produced a syringe from a cupboard of steel drawers and pumped it into my IV. My mind began to swim, but, following orders, I forced myself to keep my eyes open despite the wildly spinning room. I woke up again in a semi-private room, with Mom sitting in a chair leaning over my bed. A white curtain separated the area surrounding my bed from the rest of the room.

"There you are." Mom said, gently stroking my forehead and hairline.

She smiled lovingly, "The doctor told me everything went as expected."

She lifted the covers and examined my heavily bandaged leg. I saw that it lay in a bolster to immobilize it.

"They will wait until the swelling goes down before putting on your cast. Meanwhile, you need to keep still and give it time to heal. Are you hungry? The nurse said to push the call button when you wake up so you can get something in your stomach. She said the anesthesia was pretty rough on you, and you had a hard time coming out of it."

Though I did not feel like eating, I smiled and nodded to reassure Mom, whose face reflected concern. The bowl of Jello soothed my stinging throat, but I did not want to stay awake. Awake meant excruciating pain. I wanted to close my eyes and get out of there as soon as possible.

"S-h-h-h," I said softly as Mom started to tell me something else.

I had never shushed my mother, who we referred to as The General, but this time I did, and she heeded my request, sitting silently next to my bed. Neither had I ever attempted to spirit-travel with someone next to me, at least someone awake next to me watching closely, but I felt desperate to leave my pain and discomfort behind. I focused on the spot between my eyebrows. The morphine made the swirling light that began to emerge wavy and unstable. I saw frightening faces push in from the edges of the familiar light tunnel, reaching for me and grabbing at me from out of the darkness.

I quickly abandoned my journey, deeming it far too dangerous for my drug-altered consciousness, so I just closed my eyes and practiced thinking away the pain. I found that tapping my chest worked well to draw my attention away from my throbbing leg. Using my fingertips, I tapped firmly with a steady rhythm.

The next few days passed in a blur of painful procedures to check, clean, and rewrap my extensive wound. My right leg was unrecognizable, swollen to twice its usually swollen size, with an eight-to-ten inch incision running from several inches below my knee to well above it on the inside of my leg. The doctor ordered me to remain immobilized until the wound healed. I vaguely recall his visits when he roughly checked my progress, explaining to my mother the extensive damage he had seen in such a young joint.

After several days, I no longer received morphine and my IV was removed. It felt like Christmas when I had the use of both hands once again. I quickly learned to abandon any sense of personal dignity during that time in the hospital bed. Bedpans, sponge baths, and unwashed hair lasted for weeks.

Friends visited me from time to time. Jenny brought me an amaryllis bulb in a plastic pot. Placing it on the windowsill, she told the nurse to make sure it was watered daily. Another time my friend Michael appeared with a large orange, and a copy of *James And The Giant Peach* by Roald Dahl.

"Sorry I couldn't find a ripe peach for you to go with the book." He apologized. "It's a good story. James escapes terrible circumstances on a giant peach. That's why I wanted to bring you a peach. I wanted to help you escape." We both laughed.

Finally, after two weeks, the doctor said that my leg could be cast. This meant I would also get to leave my bed and learn to use crutches so I could go to the bathroom someplace other than my bed at last! I grew so excited when the hospital aide came in to take me to the casting room that I sat up too quickly and got a bloody nose! My trip out of bed would have to wait until the next day to my great disappointment.

Though getting my cast would open up more independence for me, it proved quite an arduous and painful ordeal. The doctor had to clean and repack my incision again—this time without the benefit of morphine. He and his assistants were too involved in the procedure to ask me to keep my eyes open, so I closed them and focused on finding that familiar light tunnel between my eyebrows. To eliminate the distracting sounds in the sterile room, I began to hum. At first, I hummed a single note. Then without planning, I found myself humming *O Susannah* as my consciousness lifted out of my body and hovered in the corner of the room where I watched myself lie there and heard the tune emerge from my physical voice. It reminded me of hearing myself moan as I came out of anesthesia, only this time I controlled it ... remotely. I could not feel what was happening to my body. I just watched as they applied layer upon layer of wet plaster gauze from the very top of my thigh all the way to my toes, completely immobilizing my entire leg, knee, ankle, and foot.

As the plaster heated up to set, I slipped back into my body and opened my eyes, still humming. A young man with a kind face smiled down at me.

"Well," he said, "I'm pretty sure that's the first time I had a patient sing *O Susannah* during a procedure!"

"It's how I focus," I told him.

"*O Susannah?*" he said with a smile.

"*O Susanna,*" I replied.

He shook his head, smiling, and prepared me to return to my room.

The next day I began twice-daily trips to physical therapy. The first time I tried to stand with crutches, the pressure of blood running into my formerly immobilized leg sent me reeling.

"Hold on there, Speedy." The therapist grabbed the belt fastened around my middle to keep me from falling over. "Just a little at a time. You've been in bed for a long while and are still weak."

Of course, he spoke the truth. I had spent nearly three weeks in that hospital bed. Every muscle had atrophied, and my stamina for even just standing had disappeared entirely. When I was not in therapy, I sat up in a chair with my leg propped up. The heavy cast made it difficult to get in or out of bed.

"Lift your leg and swing it over the side." demanded a nurse I had not seen before.

By this time, I knew everyone else on the orthopedic floor, but had never run into her. I tried to comply with every request as cheerfully as I could while in the hospital. I tried to lift my casted leg. I tried hard but could not, for the life of me, lift it.

"She looked disgusted, "You are awfully weak for someone so young. You should get more exercise at home."

Then she roughly grabbed my cast and swung it painfully over the side of the bed. My heart sank, and a large lump grew in my throat. I felt her judgment, and it brought shame. For the first time in my life, I internalized the idea of *weakness*. I had seen myself as someone with the strength to endure the many hardships I encountered in my life. I had faced things that no one, especially a sixteen-year-old, had to face. She did not know me, or my struggle, yet I heard that I needed to exercise more at home. I blamed myself for my weakness. I sank into a dark place.

That night when the only sounds came from the hallway and the nurse's station. I felt sorry for myself. I had no roommate for most of my stay, so I remained alone in my hospital room. I lay in the dim light that slipped through the slightly open door and felt like a weak, lazy, slacker. I thought about my prognosis for a painful and shortened life and began to weep silently. I pulled a pillow over my face and let the sobs be absorbed by the softness of it. My body heaved with each heart-wrenching sob until I felt exhausted. Lifting the tear-drenched pillow from my face, I took a deep breath and rubbed my eyes.

As my vision cleared, I saw a figure standing in the shadows in the corner of the room. It startled me. Thinking it was a nurse, I quickly composed myself, hoping that she had not witnessed my entire emotional breakdown. I leaned up on my elbows to say something but noticed the figure had not moved, nor made any attempt to interact with me. Looking at the figure, I soon realized it was not a nurse. A nurse would have said something or at least moved out of the shadows. I wondered if another patient had wandered into my room.

"Hello?" I said softly.

But the figure did not answer. Instead it seemed to slide backwards and slowly fade into the wall until it disappeared altogether.

I felt the familiar flutter in my gut, and a chill on the back of my neck.

"Hello," I said again, feeling a definite ethereal presence in the room with me.

"Do you need something?" The night nurse poked her head through my door.

The feeling and entity vanished instantly.

"Yes, thank you," I said. "Can I get some fresh water?"

"Sure thing Honey, I'll be right back."

She left the door open. I strained to see where the figure had stood mere seconds before, but no trace remained. Surprisingly, I felt absolutely no fear. I did not feel threatened by whatever visited me in my room and witnessed my grief. For some strange reason, its presence brought more comfort than discomfort. I slept peacefully that night.

With each day, spring continued to blossom outside the window. Days grew longer, and the sun felt warmer, brighter. The amaryllis on the windowsill grew taller and taller. I spoke words of encouragement to it every day, calling it by its name, *Amaryllis*, of course. Soon a single large bud appeared at the top of the stalk. I continued to gain strength, soon easily moving from the bed to the chair and down the hall with crutches.

One morning Mom showed up earlier than usual, followed shortly by the doctor and his regular entourage. I sat fully upright, smiling cheerfully as the doctor picked up the thick medical chart at the foot of my bed and began looking over the top of his glasses at page after page.

Then he glanced up. For the first time, he spoke directly to me instead of Mom.

"How would you like to go home today?"

I nearly leapt from the bed at the sound of those words! "Yes! Yes! I would *love* to go home today!"

Then he turned to Mom, who also smiled broadly. "Okay, Mrs. Schippers, the nurse will talk to you about what needs to happen for discharge."

He turned back to me. "Good luck, young lady. I'll see you in a week in my office."

Mom, Dr. Fahey, and his entire entourage of doctors, nurses, and medical students exited my room. I wanted to leap from the bed immediately and get dressed in the street clothes Mom had brought me in a small suitcase. As I turned to get up, I noticed *Amaryllis* on the windowsill. She displayed an enormous red blossom. I had spent nearly four weeks in hospital. Exactly the same amount of time it took for a small bulb to push up from the dirt in a plastic pot into a bright, beautiful flower.

Chapter 11: Postulant

[päs-chə-lənt] *noun*, a candidate, especially into a religious order; a person who asks or applies for something.

EACH SPRING THROUGHOUT THE REST OF MY HIGH SCHOOL YEARS brought invasive procedures on both knees. Recovery proved difficult, lengthy, and painful. I bravely endured. Soon my hands began to succumb to the ravages of my disease, causing my knuckles to stiffen and swell. I could no longer run or ride a bike. I sank into despair more than once at the loss of the activities I held dear.

One summer afternoon Up North at my grandparent's cabin, unable to go along on a walk to pick blueberries with my siblings and cousins, I sat next to Grammie Ethel's sickbed. She suffered from advanced Rheumatoid Arthritis that imprisoned her in her bed and wheelchair. She looked at me, smiled, and spoke.

"You know," she said right out of the blue, "Never make a list of things you cannot do. There's no money in that! Only make lists of what you can do. Try to find things you never would've considered when you were busy doing the things you can't."

I looked into her pale, watery blue eyes twinkling in the afternoon sunlight as I tried to decipher her meaning.

"You don't think I just stay here in this bed, now do you?"

I grew puzzled. I knew she spent time in her electric wheelchair and that Gramps took her for drives in his Lincoln, but that didn't seem to be what she meant.

"N-no, of course not ..." I stammered.

"You don't think I just stay here in this body, now do you?"

She gave me a conspiratorial wink, watching closely to see my reaction.

Does Grammie Ethel spirit-travel too? Does she know that I do? How would she know? Should I say anything about it?

"I–I don't know what you mean?"

"Of course you do." she chuckled looking away for a moment, then returning her gaze to me. "I know you know what I mean. I bet those other kids can't fly like we can."

Flabbergasted, my face lit up, and I began to laugh with Grammie Ethel. We both nodded, sharing an incredible secret that only we knew.

Grammie Ethel's wisdom pulled me out of a self-pity spiral in which I sometimes indulged. I decided I would never think about my restrictions. I would experience every day knowing that, with my troubles, came extraordinary gifts. While my friends fretted about a blemish on their faces before a big date on the weekend, I spent my time seeking the meaning of life. I searched for ways to leave the world better for my time here, no matter how little I had.

The arts provided a rewarding outlet while at the same time allowing me to keep my hands and fingers moving. I loved sculpting in clay and other pliable materials. I painted, drew, and dabbled in ceramics. I loved the entire process of creating. I played a recorder to keep my fingers supple, improvising countless melodies. I wrote poetry and prose, sang songs I learned, and composed my own.

My brother and friends played the guitar, and I sang with them every chance I got. Quickly, I learned my compromised hands made playing a guitar myself impossible. I longed to be able to accompany my own singing, but following Grammie Ethel's advice I set those thoughts aside. One day Mom came home from a craft fair carrying a strange instrument.

"I saw a man in a booth sitting in a chair and playing this," she said. "He strummed with a feather in his right hand and pressed this little wooden stick ... he said it's a "noter" I think ... Anyway, I looked at how he played, and I immediately knew you could play this ... So I bought it."

My face lit up as she handed me a beautiful, delicate, hourglass-shaped instrument.

"I've never seen one of these before. What is it?" I asked.

"It's a mountain dulcimer." She pulled a three-inch, folded pamphlet from the case, "This will tell you how to tune it and play." Barely containing her delight, she went on, "Now you can sing and play at the same time, and you can do it sitting!"

I held it in my lap and brushed the strings with a large pick that Mom also pulled from the bag. Though the untuned strings sounded discordant, to me, it was absolutely perfect. I quickly learned to tune it to itself. I used the noter to change the pitch of the first string and strummed a scale, humming each note. I only needed to press one string on different frets to play countless melodies. I now had a means of expression previously inaccessible to me. I became a musician.

•••⋮⋯⋮••

I also became a seeker of human understanding of truth and eternity. I studied world religions, cosmologies, and philosophies. I became especially enamored with the teachings and writings of Baha'u'llah and began regularly visiting the Baha'i Temple in Wilmette, Illinois. The architect had designed the structure to reflect the unity of all humankind by incorporating a vast variety of religious and architectural symbols into the design.

At the Baha'i Temple I would sit and meditate within the spacious beauty of the great rotunda. The dome gleamed white, and sparkled with quartz-laden cement. This not only made the temple appear to glow, but also seemed to charge the space, connecting me to it, and providing another gateway for my exploration beyond the corporeal. The nine pillars and sections each bore the writings of Baha'u'llah. I would lift my spirit out of my crippled body and float among the inspirational quotes.

I wondered at words and philosophy such as: *"The world of humanity has two wings – one is women and the other men. Not until both wings are equally developed can the bird fly."*

When I would leave my pain-rattled body in my bed at night to spirit-travel, I often willed myself to that temple. I felt within that space a multitude connected from around the globe and beyond visible dimensions. Frequently I saw or sensed many other energies flitting here and there within the crystal walls. I knew some belonged to living human beings. Of others, I could not be sure. They felt like energies that had never lived in a human body. I began to recognize similar energies in other places, at different times. I did not know it then, but those beings that I met in the astral dimension at the Baha'i Temple would reappear as powerful guardians and protectors later in my life.

At the same time, I also began attending local Baha'i "Firesides" where I found the deep discussions satisfying. We spoke of the truths that bind all living things. I learned that remaining open-minded toward the faiths of all humankind might bring us closer to eternal truth. I learned that the holy books around the world traced the spiritual journey of humans through time. I also learned how ritual connects us to each other and to all that is sacred.

I followed the teachings of Baha'u'llah and kept my body and mind pure, avoiding all drugs and alcohol at a time when drug use was rampant among my friends and even siblings. I observed Ramadan, fasting from sunrise to sunset for thirty days during the holy month, along with millions of others across the world. I read the Torah, the Bible, and the Quran, seeing the shared root in those religions. I learned about Buddhism, Hinduism, Shintoism, and Yoruba African ritual. I learned about how we connect to our ancestors and they to us. I learned about the natural sacred practices of indigenous people around the world and what we, in the city, could learn from them.

Grammie Ethel was right. I found something new and wonderful that I never would have discovered without my disability. I realized that my illness may have been more a blessing than a bane.

CHAPTER 12: QUEST

[kwest] *noun,* an act or instance of seeking.

IN THE FALL OF 1973, most of my friends and classmates prepared to leave for college. We had graduated together the previous spring. I continued to bear the burden of recovering from my most recent surgery, with a third planned for late winter. This, and the fact that I paid little attention to my high school academics, made any thought of university outside the realm of possibility for me. As I said goodbye to one after another of my pals who headed off to new adventures, I tried to keep Grammie Ethel's advice in mind, but it grew more and more difficult with each departure. I envisioned my future stuck at home with my seven younger siblings biding my time until my next hospitalization, isolated and friendless.

"I have a thought," Mom announced one evening.

"What?" I responded flatly.

You're turning eighteen in October." She looked at me as if waiting for a response.

"Yeah, so."

"Well, your father and I took out these Gerber Life Insurance policies for each of you kids. They mature when you turn eighteen."

"So what? Too bad I lived so long, so you can't cash in?" I laughed sarcastically.

"Of course not." She chuckled, "What I'm saying is we got them as an investment so you would have a chunk of cash when you went to college."

"Very funny," I said, swallowing the lump that grew in my throat.

"No," she went on, "Since you're not going to college this fall, why don't you use it to go on a trip?"

"A trip? Where? How"

"You know about Amtrak?" she went on. "I was just reading in the paper that you can get a three-month ticket called an AmRail Pass. You can ride as many passenger trains as you want for three months. They've been doing it in Europe for years, now we do it here too. You can visit my sister, Judy, in Colorado ... And my cousins in San Francisco and Los Angeles. I can call them to see if it's okay that you visit."

"Really?" I asked, "Alone?"

"Sure," she said. "It's safe. You'll be on a train, and you will be heading toward family."

Immediately my thinking shifted from what I could not do to the idea of a great adventure ahead. Three months would get me home well before my subsequent surgery. I could ride the rails across America to see what I might find. The next day, I took the commuter train down to Union Station and spoke to a representative at the Amtrak counter. I picked up a glossy pamphlet with all the routes and varied amenities options, spent the day at The Art Institute, and then headed back home.

A few weeks later, dressed in my travel clothes, and lace-up boots, and with a shoulder bag slung over my shoulder, I was all set. My shoulder bag contained my rail pass along with tickets for a few nights in a Pullman, or sleeper car, so I wouldn't have to sleep sitting up in the seats the whole time. It also contained a booklet of travel checks, my recorder, a box of watercolors and brushes, drawing pencils, and a small artist's journal. Mom helped me slip my arms into the canvas backpack that held everything else I would need, then wrapped her arms around me.

"Have Judy get in touch when you make it to Colorado, please. Have fun, and don't bring home any strays."

We both laughed. I had become notorious for bringing strange and wayward people home for a meal or a place to stay. I would go downtown to the Art Institute or the other museums to practice walking while recovering from surgeries, often meeting strangers and sometimes bringing them home. We always had enough food and a little extra space, despite my growing family and crowded house.

"Don't worry," I said, hugging Mom tighter. "I love you, my mama."

"I love you too, my darlin'."

Wrenching grief pierced my heart as I hugged each of my younger siblings. I had never been apart from my family for longer than my hospital stays. I also couldn't guarantee that I would see them again at all. I hadn't fully decided if I wanted to come back only to face more painful surgery and a diminishing life filled with surmounting pain. I had contemplated the possibility of an "accident" that might bring my ordeal to a close. I had planned nothing specific, but had considered the possibility. I knew from observation that life continues after our body dies. My experiences had included encountering many ghosts of the dead throughout my life. I also loved experiencing the world outside of my damaged body, in my spirit or astral body. I simply contemplated what might happen if I decided not to come back into it one time.

I made my way along the crowded platform to the train, and waited for the boarding call at four o'clock p.m. Hanging my cane over my arm, I grabbed the bars and laboriously tried to hoist myself up a formidable first step into the train car. A middle-aged porter reached for my hand and pulled me gently aboard. Deep smile lines appeared around his dark eyes, and traces of gray highlighted his closely-shorn hair.

"Good afternoon Miss!" His voice sounded like music, deep and rich. "Welcome aboard The California Zephyr! Let me help you find a seat."

Once aboard, I swung my cane off my wrist and engaged it to make my way down the aisle. The porter stopped, turned, and looked at me in exaggerated disbelief.

"What's a beautiful child like you doing with a walking stick?" He looked at my clothes and boots and went on. "It looks like you are going mountain climbing or something. Why you need that stick?"

I smiled, "Well, not for mountain climbing, that's for sure."

His warm smile met mine. "Well, Miss, you can count on Mister Robinson to take care of you while you are on my train. Now let's find you a nice spot to spend the night.

Mister Robinson found a seat near a group of other young people. He stowed my backpack above my seat, then leaned in close, saying, "I think your ride will be a little more fun around these young folks." he gestured to a small group of college-age people laughing and talking together. "Let me know if you need anything, anything at all."

He pointed forward, toward the engine, "You will find the club car in that direction." Then he pointed the other way, "And the dining car in that direction. Do you have your ticket handy?" I nodded, reaching into my shoulder bag. "Good," he said "the conductor will be by in a few minutes to check your ticket. How far you goin'?

"I'm not altogether certain," I said, "I've got an Amrail pass, but my first stop is Denver."

"Well, Miss," He smiled, "enjoy your ride on my train tonight."

Pressing my forehead against the glass, I watched Chicago slip past the window of the train car, craning my neck to spot familiar buildings and taking in every sight, planting them firmly in my memory. Before long, I turned my head around to see where we were headed, looking forward to whatever unknown adventure lay before me. I rummaged in my shoulder bag, found my notebook and a drawing pencil, and quickly sketched the train car with the tops of heads peeking above the seat backs. I added houses and trees in the windows, then rubbed my finger across the soft graphite to blur the image as it appeared from the moving train. Next, I wrote my thoughts in a few lines of poetry.

Just as I finished the first page of my travel diary, a young woman popped up from the seat in front of me and introduced herself. She had wild curly dark hair and olive skin. Her black eyes shone under a thick brow. She wore a baggy peasant shirt, torn jeans, and many bangles and necklaces.

"You from Chicago?" she asked.

I nodded.

"We're from Ann Arbor. We just crashed for a few days in Chicago. I heard you say you had an Amrail pass. We do too."

Several other hippie-looking folks began to congregate around my seat.

"We are heading to the club car for some sandwiches and beers. Wanna come with?"

"Sure," I said, closing my sketch diary and tucking it into my shoulder bag. "Thanks."

They all watched as I grabbed my cane from under the seat.

"Are you some kind of cripple?" asked one of the young men.

"Jesus, Jimmy!" admonished another, "Don't be an asshole! Do you need a hand?" he asked, smiling sweetly.

"No thanks, I've got it," I replied, trying to move as gracefully as possible.

"Go ahead," he said, motioning for me to walk in front of him as the others hurried off.

"I'm Mike."

I wished he would've gone ahead of me. I knew that the moving train would make my unstable gait even more pronounced. I didn't want to appear more crippled than had already been announced.

"Thanks," I said sheepishly. "I'm Tiyi."

We had to pass between the train cars. I hadn't anticipated just how treacherous an endeavor it would prove with the floor moving side to side beneath my feet. As I tried to navigate, my knees buckled. I tightly gripped my cane and reached out for the walls to keep from crashing to the floor. Mike quickly reached out and held me up.

"Careful!" he said, putting his hands on my waist, "I've got you. Let me get that door."

He shifted his position and moved beside me, putting one arm firmly around my waist while reaching for the sliding door with the other.

"I'm sorry," I said, blushing. "I'm so clumsy."

"Actually you're pretty amazing," he said with his face so close I could feel the heat of it on my skin, "and beautiful."

"C'mon," he quickly added, blushing himself, "Let's catch up to the others."

We had to pass between several other train cars. Each time Mike put his arm firmly around me to help me pass safely. When we reached the club car at last, he sat close to me on a bench.

The others had already ordered beers. Mike offered to buy me one, but I declined, telling them that I was a Baha'i and didn't drink alcohol. Instead, he ordered two cans of ginger ale, one for me and one for him. I felt grateful for his kind gesture.

The others wanted to know what Baha'i meant. I explained what I knew of the teachings of Baha'u'llah. Mike put his arm around me on the back of the bench. As the others drank more, they became louder and more boisterous. Hours had passed when the bartender, a young black man, announced that he had to close up the club car. The dark-haired girl flirted with him and asked if he could lock up, but let us hang out there for a while. She produced a joint from the pocket of her jeans.

"We can share."

He smiled, turned down the lights, and locked the door. Then he put more beers on the bar and said, "I can share too!"

Mike and I spoke softly while the others sought complete inebriation. Somewhere in Nebraska or Kansas, the bartender announced that we all needed to leave so he could clean up before the sun came up or somebody would fire his ass.

The group staggered from the club car, strewn with empty beer cans and cigarette butts, with the odor of weed hanging in the air.

"Can we help?" I asked when the others had gone.

"Sweet Jesus! I'm gonna be fired for sure," the bartender said, looking at the carnage and shaking his head.

"We will help," Mike offered, gathering up some empty cans.

"Thanks, man." he shook his head, "What was I thinking?"

I opened a window slightly to clear the stale air, then picked up butts, and spent roaches from the table and ashtrays in the arms of the seats. My head swam from both the side smoke and exhaustion.

"Thanks, friends," said the bartender, "I got it from here. You two head back to your seats and get some rest.

Mike kept his arm around me as we carefully made our way back to our car. The others lay sprawled in various states of undress across each other and the seats.

"Mind if I sit with you?" he asked.

"Please," I replied, sliding in next to the window.

We whispered as the sky turned from black to violet with streaks of magenta spreading out across the sparse clouds. We discussed our lives and dreams. He told me that he and his friends had decided to take a semester off from the University of Michigan to travel on the trains together. I told him about my situation and what lay ahead of me. When he expressed pity for my disability and struggles, I told him what Grammie Ethel had told me.

"You don't think I just stay here in this ravaged body, now do you?"

His brow furrowed in bewilderment. I explained how I had learned to separate my soul from my body and spirit-travel. He listened attentively and asked if I could teach him. I explained how to focus on his spirit energy and push it out of his physical body. We practiced positioning the palms of our hands near one another, closing our eyes, and focusing on sensing the energy of the other, then pulling them further apart. The rhythmic motion of the train, the long day, and the late hour began to take their toll.

Soon my eyelids grew heavy, and I felt myself drifting off. I sighed deeply and leaned onto Mike's shoulder. As I slipped into sleep, I felt his gentle kiss on my hairline. Though I did not want the night to end, I could fight sleep no longer.

I awoke groggy, still leaning on Mike, with the sapphire sky and bright sun shining above the speeding train.

"Did you sleep at all?" I asked, sitting up and attempting to loosen my stiff body.

"Not really," he said. "Check that out."

Turning toward the window, I gasped at the sight of the Rocky Mountains rising in the distance from a vast, flat, desolate plain. I had never seen mountains like that. I had expected to be amazed, but the juxtaposition of the flat earth and the distant mountains rendered me gobsmacked.

Mike leaned close to gaze out the window with me.

"Pretty cool, eh?" he said.

When I turned to answer he leaned in with a soft, lingering kiss. I closed my eyes and let the warmth and sweetness of it wash over me.

"Why don't you just stay with us?" he asked. "It would be a blast to travel these next months together, wouldn't it?"

Catching my breath, I considered his tempting offer.

"I can't," I replied. "My uncle is meeting me in Denver. I'm going to stay with him and my aunt in a tiny cabin without running water or electricity in the mountains. I will never have a chance to do something like that again."

"Maybe," he kissed me once more, "But I will never see you again if you do."

"Don't be so sure," I replied. "Remember, I don't stay in this body."

"I like this body," he said, wrapping his arms around me. "I think you should stay on the train."

"Ha!" I laughed, "This body is a hindrance, and it's going to spend a week or two on a mountainside."

We sat holding hands for the next few hours until the conductor walked through, announcing the next stop, Denver. Mike helped me gather my things as the train pulled into the station, and came to a lurching stop.

"You sure?" he asked with pleading eyes.

"Farewell," I said, kissing him one last time. "I'll see you in my dreams. You can come too, you know."

Turning to the rest of my newfound friends, I waved goodbye and then made my way to the exit without looking back. I could feel Mike's eyes on me as the sliding door closed behind me.

That night, tucked under heavy quilts in the tiny mountain cabin, I closed my eyes and visualized the train car and Mike. As the log fire in the stove turned to embers, I sent my spirit to that train where I saw Mike curled up and sleeping soundly on the seat.

Told you. I thought.

Chapter 13: Allies

[a-ˌlīs] *noun*, a person or group that provides assistance
and support in an ongoing struggle

AFTER TEN DAYS IN A SNOWY MOUNTAIN CABIN with Judy and Dave, the time
came for me to move on to my next destination. Though the scenery
proved idyllic and the company delightful, I knew that I needed to give
their space back to them. Judy, several months pregnant, worked every
waking minute to keep the cabin warm and food on the table. Though I
pitched in as best I could, I began to get in the way.

They agreed to drive me to the train. This meant leaving by 5:30
a.m. to make our way down the mountain arriving for an 8:00 a.m.
departure to Salt Lake City. Though Dave did not look forward to the
early morning drive over treacherous snow-covered roads, Judy expressed
excitement for going to the city to do some shopping and maybe lunching
in a cafe.

When we arrived at the station, I thanked them and assured them
I could find my way to the platform, encouraging them not to bother
parking, but just drop me off. After many warm hugs and kisses, I made
my way into the station. I had booked this particular train intentionally
for this next leg of my journey. It followed the Denver and Rio Grande
Western Railroad track, well known for its remarkable scenery. We
would leave the station at eight in the morning and arrive in Salt Lake
City after eleven the same night. Though the train would continue to
San Francisco, my next destination, I decided to get off for the night and

find a motel room where I could sleep in a comfortable bed and take a proper shower.

I checked in at the counter, took a seat on a well-worn wooden bench in the waiting area and pulled out my sketch diary. I had filled many pages during my stay with Judy, but I wanted to write a few reflections. Looking up, I noticed an elderly couple snuggling on a bench across the room. I felt a pang of jealousy, then deep sorrow watching them holding hands and whispering lovingly to one another. I had just spent more than a week with Judy and Dave, who were expecting their first child. Their whole happy life as a family lay ahead of them. Now I witnessed this elderly couple who had obviously spent decades loving one another. My heart filled with longing.

I will never have a family, I thought. *I will grow more and more crippled as my short life progresses. I should've taken Mike's offer and stayed on the train.*

I took an empty seat and put my backpack on the seat across and facing me hoping to avoid having to share the space with another traveler. I did not feel like talking to anyone. I just wanted to be alone to feel sorry for myself. I thought hard about options to stop the inevitable progression of time.

The elderly couple took the seat on the opposite side of the train, one seat ahead, facing me, so I could not avoid watching how much they loved each other. It made me sad, then angry. I mourned a future I thought I would never have. Watching them felt like God or the universe was rubbing it in my face.

Two young men wearing large cowboy hats, jeans, and cowboy boots took the seat directly across the aisle from me. They both tipped their hats and said "Ma'am" as they took their seats

The fifteen-hour trek took us through arguably the most beautiful scenery in North America. The track was hewn from the walls of Glenwood Canyon along the snaking Feather River far below. I soon forgot about my self pity and watched in amazement as the canyon wall flew by on the left, and a cliff fell to the river on the right.

The opposite side of the canyon seemed close enough to reach out and touch. I had no time to paint as one awe-inspiring thing after another flew past the window, so I roughed in sketches as quickly as I could. Several times the elderly man left his seat to walk past me down the aisle, presumably to use the restroom. Every time he slowed, smiling warmly, making sure our eyes met.

Suddenly the cowboys stood up excitedly, and pointed through my window toward an enormous golden eagle sitting on a nest on the far wall of the canyon, maybe twenty feet away but distanced by a drop of thousands of feet. Everyone in the car quickly rose to witness the majesty of a rare creature close to extinction.

"I noticed your drawing, ma'am." Said one of the young men. "You do pretty good."

"Nah," I replied, closing my sketchbook, "It's only for me to remember my trip."

"I like it too, ma'am" said the other, leaning around his companion and grinning.

They had both removed their hats and stood in the aisle next to my bench, smiling sheepishly at me.

"Thank you," I replied, blushing slightly.

"Mind if we join you?"

I moved my backpack from the seat across from me and motioned for them to sit down. I noticed the elderly couple both watching and smiling in approval.

The cowboys informed me that they were brothers from outside of Salt Lake City. They had gone to Denver for business regarding their family's ranch.

"So you don't just dress like cowboys. You actually *are* cowboys!" I chuckled, "Boys I grew up with like to wear cowboy hats and pretend, but it looks like you boys are the real deal!"

They laughed and nodded. We enjoyed the scenery together for several hours, laughing and comparing my stories of growing up in Chicago with theirs of growing up on a ranch in Utah. After sunset, the only thing visible in the window was the reflection of the people on the train.

"I'm getting pretty hungry," one said to his brother. "Suppose we go and get some grub?" Then, turning to me asked, "Would you like to join us in the dining car?"

"Thank you, no," I replied, "I'm on a tight budget, and the dining car is pretty pricey. I'll grab a sandwich in the club car."

The elderly couple made their way arm in arm past my seat on their way to their dinner, again slowing and smiling at me. They seemed so familiar somehow, though I could not recall from where.

"Pardon me, ma'am, but I wouldn't have invited you if I wasn't planning on paying for your meal."

"Thank you," I repeated, " but I can't let you do that."

"Well, gee ma'am," the other brother said, "it would make my dinner a whole lot more pleasurable if you were there. I see my big brother all the time. Please be our guest. We are not on a tight budget, and I, for one, would love nothing more than to have a pretty lady to look at across the table instead of my ugly big brother."

Succumbing to their charm, I relented and joined them for dinner. I liked them both. Their disarming shyness and easy way of teasing one another added to their appeal. They shared vivid stories of a world I could never imagine, filling the remaining hours with affection and laughter. I attempted to paint a portrait of the two of them wearing their cowboy hats, but it turned out more abstract than not. They gushed over it anyway and wrote their names and address on that page in my sketchbook.

As we grew close to the end of the journey, I asked if they knew of a motel near the depot where I could spend the night, sleep in a bed, and shower before catching the next train to San Francisco the following day.

"Yes, ma'am," the older brother declared. "The train depot isn't in a very nice part of town, and we won't get there until almost midnight. We'd be happy to make sure you get to a motel all safe and sound."

At the station, I noticed the elderly couple remained in their seats, leaning on one another. The woman dozed, but the man caught my eye one last time and nodded, smiling. I smiled and nodded back.

The cowboys helped me off the train and would not allow me to carry my things. One carried my backpack and the other my shoulder bag as we walked two blocks to a sketchy-looking motel with a red neon sign flashing VACANCY. For the first time on my journey, I felt vulnerable as the older brother approached the desk, paid for the room, and pocketed the key. I hoped I had not misread them and that they had nothing sordid in mind, but reminded myself that in all my years of bringing home strangers—"strays" as my mother called them—I hadn't misread anyone yet. All trepidation melted away as he handed me the key and walked me to my door.

"Be sure to lock up tight now, ma'am, and don't answer the door for anybody until morning."

They took a step back and tipped their hats as I thanked them and closed the door to my first very own motel room.

"Cowboys." I announced to the empty room, chuckling to myself, then headed to the shower.

••••:·••:•••

After a long hot shower, I climbed between the cool, clean sheets and slept well into the late morning. I needed to check out, then find something to do until I could catch the train to San Francisco, leaving at 11:30 p.m. Donning my backpack and shoulder bag, I set out into west Salt Lake City. I did not know the city, and saw no way to find out, so I made sure to keep track of the way back to the train depot.

Soon I came upon a small corner diner, bustling with a lunchtime crowd. Locating a tiny booth, I sat down and pulled my sketch journal out of my shoulder bag. I was looking at the menu when the waitress, a no-nonsense middle-aged woman, took my order. I first made sure she would honor traveler's checks. I ordered a sandwich, hot tea, and two glasses of water. When she looked at me, puzzled, I showed her my sketch journal and paint box. She smiled and nodded, then turned to walk away.

Waiting for my lunch, I began adding color to some of the quick sketches I had made of the canyon and river the day before. I painted page after page, stopping only to take a small bite from time to time.

As the lunch crowd waned, the waitress came to my booth.

"More hot water?" She asked, noticing my empty cup.

"Yes, please," I replied, "And... would you mind getting me a fresh glass of water too?" Indicating the muddy paint water.

"Only if you show me what you are doing." She said with a wink.

I turned the book around so she could have a look.

"Wow. That's some pretty country? Haven't seen you around here before. What brought you?"

"The train," I replied.

"Well, Honey, I figured that out from your pictures and the fact that the station is only a couple of blocks away. What I'm asking is why are you all alone?"

I told her how I got my rail pass. I told her where I had come from and why I traveled alone. I told her about my family, my impairment, and my pending surgery. I told her that it would probably be the only chance I would ever have to travel like this because I would soon lose the ability to do anything alone as my disease progressed. I have no idea why I told her so much. She never asked for the story of my life and my tribulations. It all came pouring out that afternoon in a diner west of downtown Salt Lake City, Utah.

She listened without a word, then sat down in the seat across from me. Folding her hands on the table, she gazed so deeply into my eyes that I felt tears begin to well up. I blinked hard, attempting to mask my vulnerability. Her expression grew gentle as she tilted her head slightly to one side. Her eyes softened, and a slight smile appeared. I sat silently, forcing the throb of self-pity down my throat, and into my chest.

"You're so lucky." She said.

My confusion began to morph into anger.

Lucky? I thought. *How could she possibly think that?*

"Sounds like you have a pretty smart mama." She added. "I sure wish someone had helped me take my last chance at freedom."

Her face lit up with a full-on grin. She winked and said, rising from her seat, "Stay as long as you like. I know your train leaves late. We're open all night."

Watching her walk away, I wondered about her story, contemplating what chances she might have missed. Still, I did not feel all that lucky.

I continued to paint and write a few lines of poetry. Later, she unceremoniously set a slice of apple pie on my table. I looked up to thank her, but she had already turned away. Several times she dropped a fresh glass of paint water, taking away the dirty water, and brought me a fresh teabag and hot water. As the diner began to fill for the dinner rush, I watched her expertly serve table after table, laughing and joking with the diners. I sketched and painted a scene with her leaning over a table to pour coffee into a cup, then added several lines of poetry, stealthily covering it as she passed so she would not see it.

The sky outside the diner window began to turn purple as she brought me the blue plate special.

"Here you go, Honey," she said, "Eat up, then you should get back to the station, so you don't have to walk alone in the pitch dark."

I thanked her, packed up my things, and polished off the delicious meal. Then I asked for my check.

"On the house, Honey. Think about me sometimes on your trip, and it'll almost be like I'm riding the train too."

She accepted no argument, holding her hand up as she turned and walked away briskly. Feeling surprised and uncomfortable with her kindness and wanting a way to thank her, I knew what to do. I signed the painting I had made of the diner, tore it out of my journal, and left it on the table.

"Thank you!" I called as I walked through the door. "Thank you."

◆••᛫᛫•᛫᛫᛫•᛫•◆

Arriving at the depot two hours before my train, I spread out on a wooden bench, and rested my head on my backpack. A security cop approached me.

"You can't sleep here tonight." He said gruffly.

When I showed him my ticket, he scowled and walked away. Between my experiences with the cowboys and the waitress, I had begun to think that everybody in Salt Lake City had a heart of gold. The security guard proved that assumption false.

At last, I boarded the *California Zephyr* for the next leg of my journey. It would be a two-day ride. I had booked a Pullman car for the nights ahead. The porter carried my backpack and led me to the tiny cabin.

"Here you go Miss. Would you like me to pull down your bunk?"

"Yes, thank you, I replied. My body ached with exhaustion.

"Why don't you take a seat in the coach so I can make it nice for you, okay, Miss?" He flashed me a warm smile.

I agreed and managed to make my way safely to a seat in the adjacent car before the train began to move. I noticed the same elderly couple from the day before. I had not noticed them getting off the train in Salt Lake City and just assumed they had gone on to California, but there they sat, sleeping in each other's arms as if they had never moved. I stared at them, bewildered. All at once, the gentleman looked up, catching my gaze with his piercing blue eyes, and smiled. Embarrassed, I smiled back just as the porter arrived to escort me to my bunk. I felt the old man's eyes on my back as I walked away.

Lying on the bunk in the small compartment, I watched through a slit in the window blind as the world rushed past. The rhythmic clicking of steel wheels on a steel track accentuated by an occasional train whistle served as a perfect lullaby, and I fell into a deep, restful sleep.

The train came to a lurching stop. I awoke with no idea of the time or where we had landed. After a bagel and coffee in the club car, I decided to sit in the coach instead of my Pullman car to take advantage of the bigger windows through which I could watch the scenery. "Good morning." I greeted the elderly couple who remained in the seat where I had seen them the night before.

"Good morning to you," replied the gentleman as his wife smiled warmly.

"I noticed your painting. I like your work."

"Thanks," I replied, "I'm not very good."

"I am." He said, "I'm a retired art professor. Watercolor is my primary medium."

My cheeks grew hot with embarrassment.

"You've got all the right instincts," he said. "Would you have any interest in a few tips and techniques? I'd love to help you on your way."

"Yes, please," I said, nodding.

He motioned for me to sit in the seat facing them, then got up to sit alongside me.

"Show me what you've been doing." He said.

I handed him my journal. He thumbed through it, stopping at each page to examine my work. Watching his face and expression closely, I grew more self-conscious.

"Looks like you've got all the basics down. Did you figure this out for yourself, or have you had classes?"

"I took art class in high school but mostly just played with it."

"That's great," he smiled broadly. "Played with it. I like it. That's what makes an artist. Would you like to learn a few brush techniques that I bet will open up a lot of possibilities for you?"

He showed me how to prepare the dry paint to get the most out of the pigments, load different brushes for different effects, and multiple wet and dry techniques. I loved how just a few adjustments enhanced the quality of my work enormously.

After the lesson, he returned to his place next to his wife as we chatted, marveling at how train travel brought unlikely strangers together. I remarked that, on a train, the trip itself was the adventure, not the destination. They lovingly considered one another and smiled.

"Of course, you need to have a lot of time on your hands, though," I said.

"Time," he repeated sadly. "Time is so precious." He reached for his wife's hand, then looked deeply into my eyes. "Every single minute, no matter how painful or difficult … every living minute is a most precious gift."

That's easy for you to say, I thought, my eyes welling up with tears, *You both had a long life filled with someone you love deeply. You have no idea what kind of struggle and pain I have endured and will experience in the short life the fates have dealt me. I'm not sticking around for that ordeal.*

"You know," he studied my expression, "It really doesn't matter how many minutes one has. It matters only what you do with them, what you learn from them."

He turned to his wife as she closed her eyes and lay her head on his shoulder.

"When we got Mary's cancer diagnosis, we knew that our time grew limited with each passing day. Instead of enduring painful and fruitless medical treatment that might keep her alive an extra month at best, we decided to get the train pass to spend as much time as possible in each other's arms traveling to places neither of us had ever seen. We are going to stay on the train making new memories until the cancer makes it impossible to go on. So you see. Every single living moment is indeed a precious gift … when … If you live them mindfully, you can not even imagine what wonders they may reveal."

Though his story was theirs, I knew in my very bones that the message was intended for me. I felt that he somehow knew I had considered ending my life before it became too difficult. I felt ashamed at my jealousy of them, and of my weakness and unwillingness to trust the path that lay before me. I felt no need to tell my story or reveal my own troubles. Instead, I bathed in the warmth of their love and kindness. That was enough.

That night, lying in my bunk, I reflected on what I had learned. I resolved to live the life before me as mindfully as possible, choosing joy instead of despair, love instead of fear, and treating every living moment as a gift.

The next morning I dressed, packed my things, and returned to the coach to find my new friends. I saw no sign of them, so I made my way to the diner. When I didn't find them there, I went to the club car. Still no luck. I checked different cars, wondering if they decided to go to one of the vista cars with top seating to view the landscape. With only an hour left before I would leave the train, I could not find them anywhere. I began to worry, wondering if something had happened to Mary over-night that forced them off the train. I asked the conductor if they had gotten off the train at one of the overnight stops.

He seemed confused, saying that he did not recall such a couple. I asked if he had been on the train all night, and he said he had. This confused and worried me even more. Pulling my journal from my bag, I looked back at the pages to make sure the previous day hadn't been a dream. It seemed so weird how I had seen them between Denver and Salt Lake City, then again the next day on the train between Salt Lake and San Francisco despite me getting off the train and on another the following day. It just didn't make sense.

Still, there in my journal, I saw the pages with his brush mark-ings and saw the way I had altered my previous paintings using the tech-niques he had taught me. Our encounter *had* happened. It had proved life-changing for me, and yet I could not unequivocally decipher whether they were real. Had someone or something dropped angels in my path to keep me focused? Either way, it worked. I continued my quest with a new willingness and a new acceptance of every minute before me.

Chapter 14: Adrift

[ə-'drift n] *adverb*; without motive power and without anchor or mooring

When I returned home after my adventure, I had months before my next surgery, so I returned to my job at a high-end toy store in an antique tourist shopping area near my home. I focused on work and family but felt increasingly disconnected. It seemed as though my real life circled around me in a holding pattern somewhere just out of reach. I knew more loomed somewhere beyond my comprehension. I wanted to remain ready.

Surgery again put me back in a wheelchair and on crutches. I practiced new ways to manage the pain, finding that playing my dulcimer immersed my mind and body in the vibration of the strings. When I added my voice, it left no room for pain or suffering. Music created a sacred space for me, and I went there often.

I spent spring and summer recovering and regaining my strength and mobility. In August, my friend, Elise, asked if I wanted to move to Michigan with her. She wanted to work to establish residency since out-of-state tuition made it impossible for her to afford to return in the fall.

I thought about it for mere seconds, then agreed. I had a small nest-egg saved from my job and had recovered enough to make the move.

Weeks later, we found a tiny, one-bedroom apartment carved out of an old house in a seedier part of Lansing where we set up housekeeping. I found a job almost immediately at a toy and hobby store in a strip mall not too far from our apartment. I grew to love the owner and my coworkers. When Lew, the owner, learned that I sometimes hitchhiked to work in the mornings, he insisted that he pick me up at my house instead.

We had no phone or TV and mainly ate macaroni and cheese from a box, or noodles prepared in as many ways as we could conjure. We made soup and beans and rice and survived on a tiny income, but we had fun.

Elise had many friends in the area that she had met at Michigan State (MSU) the previous year. We attended lots of parties and went to hear bands play in East Lansing on two-dollar-pitcher nights. I met many interesting people and became completely preoccupied with the life of a young single woman in the mid-seventies.

One night at a party I encountered a young man with long, unkempt hair, a scraggly beard, and eastern-looking clothing. He sat in the middle of a gathering of mostly young women preaching about all things metaphysical and spiritual. This was right in my wheelhouse after years of studying world religions through the lens of my Catholic girls' high school religion classes, the teachings of Baha'u'llah, and my experience in the spirit world. I loved conversations on these topics and joined in.

Soon we found ourselves debating the nature of spirit, the dichotomy of the human spirit, and physical life. After an intriguing exchange I excused myself to mingle among other friends at the party. The young man followed close behind, continuing to try to engage. I politely tried to discourage him, inserting myself into other conversations, but he would not let up.

During one of those conversations, another guest remarked that he had seen me where I worked. He said that he worked in a shop in that same strip mall. I told him that I worked in the toy store. We made plans to meet for lunch one day the following week. As I turned to find a fresh drink, I noticed the creepy man standing off a bit glaring at me, so I made my way to the kitchen. He followed and cornered me by the back door, moving in a little too close for comfort. I began to see something crazy in his eyes.

His smile grew sinister as he said, "I've been waiting for you."

"I just wanted to get something to drink," I replied nervously.

"No," he whispered, "I mean, I've been waiting for you to come into my life."

Assuming he was feeding me a pick-up line, I laughed, rolled my eyes, and shook my head.

He grew annoyed, "You don't understand ..." He moved even closer. "The Lord told me you would come to me. It's been ordained."

I grew more uncomfortable, wishing someone who knew me would come into the kitchen to extricate me from this precarious situation.

"Ordained by whom?" I tried to find a way around him and back to the room filled with people.

"By The Lord God,"

Now the crazy in his eyes took on an even more sinister glare.

"You are mistaken," I said, pushing around him toward the dining room.

"God is speaking now. It's our destiny. We will be together forever." he reached out to grab me.

"No." I said forcefully, pushing past him, "I don't know which god you have in your head, but my god has other plans for me, and so do I."

I left him standing alone in the kitchen and made sure I stayed in a large group of familiar friends for the duration of the evening, until I saw him leave.

Having no car, Elise usually managed to bum a ride from other party-goers, but this time we stayed until all the folks we could ask had already left, so she and I set out to walk several blocks home to our apartment.

Elise asked me about the guy she saw talking to me. I told her that he had creeped me out. I said it started out fun, since I love talking about spooky and spiritual things. Then he got crazy.

As we walked along the main street well after midnight, I began to feel uneasy. With nearly three blocks left, I glanced behind us and saw him walking in our direction ... Less than a block behind us.

"Jesus Christ!" I said, "I think he's following us."

Elise turned around and said, "Maybe he lives this way too."

"No way." I said, growing more fearful, "He left more than an hour ago. What if he was waiting for me to leave?"

"Let's just get home and lock the door. Maybe he won't follow when we turn the corner."

We picked up our pace as best I could, arriving at our apartment in minutes. My heart sank as I saw him turn the corner down our street just as we climbed to the porch.

"Jesus!" I said, "He saw where we live! Let's not turn on the light yet, so he at least doesn't know which apartment we are in."

Elise agreed. We securely locked the front and back doors, then went quietly into the bedroom, getting undressed in the dark. I barely slept that night, listening for the sound of someone trying to break in. At last, as the morning light slipped into the room, I fell into a fitful sleep.

When the clock radio alarm woke me, I was alone in the apartment. Elise worked two jobs, and had already left. I took a shower, unable to shake the feeling that something dangerous lurked nearby. Nervously, I dressed and had a cup of tea and a piece of toast.

Lew, my boss, didn't work that day, so I had promised to take the bus. I counted out the correct change for my fare, grabbed my shoulder bag and keys, and left through the front door. As I turned the key to lock it, I saw him standing by the side of the house, just off the porch.

"Good morning," he said.

My heart pounded, but I refused to make eye contact with him. I began walking as quickly as possible down the sidewalk toward my bus stop. He followed behind, trying to engage me by quoting scripture. I completely ignored him, calling on my allies and angels to protect me. I maintained a sense of his distance in case he attempted to catch up to do me harm. Though terrified, I held a posture of control and power with every step.

As I approached the bus stop, I felt relieved that others were waiting on the corner for the bus. I walked directly into the middle of the group.

"Hey," he said, "You can't just walk away from destiny."

"Leave me alone," I said firmly, backing up as he moved closer.

A large black man waiting for the bus asked, "Are you okay?"

I shook my head, *no* as my stalker said, "It's okay. We are together."

"NO, WE ARE NOT!" I raised my voice in a fury.

As he reached out to grab my arm, the stranger stepped up.

"Back off, man!" he bellowed, stepping between my stalker and me. "Leave the young lady alone!"

He lightly shoved my stalker back as the bus arrived, then motioned for me to board ahead of him, turning to prohibit my tormentor from boarding behind us.

Relieved beyond measure, I thanked the gentleman.

"You know that crazy dude?" he asked.

"I just met him last night," I replied.

"Miss," he went on, "Don't bring crazy guys like that home."

"I didn't," I began to explain, but then reconsidered, realizing that my own actions had drawn him to me in the first place. I had playfully enjoyed debating topics that he clearly found deadly serious. Feeling I was to blame for this predicament, I realized what my protector thought of me—somebody who brought strange men home. I thanked him, sat sheepishly, and reflected on my social habits until our bus reached my stop.

Once at work, I made myself busy trying to forget about the events of the prior night and morning, but grew unnerved when I spotted him outside in the parking lot walking toward the shop.

The mall had a long enclosed corridor that sheltered all the entrances to the shops. He walked up to the outer glass, facing the toy store, stretched out his arms, and put his hands on the outer glass in a crucifixion pose.

My breath caught in my throat. He tipped his head to one side with a pleading expression on his face.

"Oh my God!" I gasped.

"What?" Dirk, the manager, saw my face go ashen. He sensed my fear, then looked in the direction of my stare.

"Who is that?" he asked, scowling.

"Some guy I saw at a party last night," my eyes fixed on the form attached to the outer glass. "He followed me home. Elise and I locked him out, but he was there again this morning when I left for work. He followed me to the bus stop, but I thought I lost him there."

Suddenly I realized that he must have overheard my conversation about where I worked. Tears filled my eyes.

"Are you dating this guy?" Dirk asked, not taking his eyes off of the strange spectacle on the glass.

"NO!" I insisted, "I don't even know his name! He just latched on to me. He's scaring me."

Dirk, a sergeant in the Marine Reserves, stood six feet four. He had broad shoulders and, though a sweetheart, projected a powerful demeanor when he chose to wield it.

"I'll take care of this," he said, striding aggressively out the door.

I watched him loom over the other man. Though I could not hear what he said, he appeared to be barking orders. My tormentor looked tiny next to him, and continued to shrink with the onslaught. After several minutes, I watched him slink away while Dirk stood watching with his hands on his hips.

"I don't think he'll be back," he said, returning to the shop.

"What did you say?" asked Alana, another girl who worked there.

"Doesn't matter." he said, "Let's get back to business here. There's stock that needs pricing."

Later, Dirk insisted that he drive me home. He lived in the opposite direction. I thanked him, starting to protest, but one look from him told me that I had no choice in the matter. I felt relieved because I knew that tonight Elise had to work late waiting tables, and I would be home alone all evening without a phone.

After closing up, we headed to the parking lot. I scanned the entire area but did not see my stalker. Dirk had a big black pickup truck. As we turned out of the mall parking lot, I saw my tormentor lurking at the bus stop where I would have caught my bus home. I shrank down in the seat so he could not see me.

When we arrived at my apartment, Dirk waited in the truck.

"Lock your doors," he ordered, "and next time, don't talk to crazy strangers."

"Thanks." I said and hurried inside, locking the door behind me.

I stayed in the back of the house and kept the lights off, figuring that eventually that guy would figure out I had left work. I wanted him to think I had not gone home if he came creeping around my house.

When I heard the keys at the front door, I nearly jumped out of my skin. Elise was home.

I asked her if she saw that guy lurking outside either in the morning or when she got home. She said she hadn't. I told her about the incident at work.

"Maybe we should call the police," she said.

I shot her a side-eye. "Phone?" I asked incredulously. We didn't have a phone.

"No, I mean tomorrow ... from work."

"I doubt he will come back to my work after Dirk read him the riot act," I replied.

"Well," said Elise climbing into the bed we shared, "Maybe he will just give up."

"Hope so," I said, turning over to try to sleep.

I grabbed my bag and jacket when I heard Lew honk his car horn twice, our signal that he had arrived to drive me to work. As I exited the front door, I thought I spotted a figure slip around the side of the house just out of sight. My hair stood on end as I sensed danger, but I hoped it was just a wayward spirit attached to the house. I had sensed something there before, but never felt threatened by it, figuring it to be nothing more than residual energy in the old house's walls. I made my way to the car waiting at the curb. As we drove away, I turned to look back toward my house, and there I saw my stalker standing just under my bedroom window, watching us drive away. I would have much preferred a ghost to the living danger that lurked there.

I should have said something to Lew, but didn't. My fear grew, but I still blamed myself. The way Dirk had admonished me to not talk to crazy strangers, along with the way the man at the bus stop judged me, made me feel that I had somehow brought this on myself. My arrogance in spouting my knowledge of spirit, religions, and history had come back to bite me. I thought that I should have just kept my mouth shut. My ego and naivete had put me in danger. Real danger.

After lunch, I looked out the front display window. Terror gripped my soul as I saw him leaning against a light post halfway across the parking lot. Dirk had the day off, and nothing about Lew's small stature made him intimidating.

Alana, my coworker, noticed my concern and asked what had happened. I pointed to the man in the parking lot.

"Lew!" she shouted frantically toward the office, "Come here quick!"

Lew, sensing trouble, raced from the back.

Seeing no one in the shop, he asked, slightly annoyed, "What?"

Alana indicated the guy in the lot. Much to my chagrin, she told him the whole story.

Lew looked at me with fatherly concern. "Well! That's enough of this."

He went to the phone and called the police.

Within minutes two officers entered the store and interviewed me. I told them everything: how he followed me home, lurked under my window, and hid beside my porch. I was sure to include my stalker's telling me that God told him our union was ordained ...The whole sordid tale.

Alana looked on, horrified.

"Not much we can do since he never actually trespassed." said one officer to Lew, closing his notepad. "We will chat with him, try to scare him off, but other than that, he hasn't committed a crime. What's your address, Miss? We can try to have a unit swing past your house tonight if you like."

Discouraged, I flatly said, "Thanks, hopefully, that will help," knowing it would not dissuade that man from following what he thought God had ordained.

We watched from the shop as the police carried on a conversation with my stalker. I saw them writing in their notebook.

Maybe they are getting his name, so they have a suspect after he murders me. I thought helplessly.

He walked away in the opposite direction from my house, before the police left. We all watched him go, then settled back into our work. I hoped that the efforts of Dirk and the officers might have convinced him to leave me alone, but truly doubted it.

After we closed the shop, Lew drove me to the market so I could get some groceries, then drove me home and parked on a side street next to my house. Lew got out with me and walked all around the building, making sure nobody lurked anywhere. We looked up and down the streets in all directions. When he felt certain that my stalker was not outside, Lew walked me to my door, waiting to make sure I was safe.

"Go in and lock up before I leave." He said. I'm going to sit here in my car for a few minutes just for my peace of mind."

You don't have to do that," I protested, "He's no place in sight."

"Either way," he said, waving me off as he made his way to his car. "I'll see you in the morning."

"Thank you so much!" I called as I closed and locked my front door.

I spent another sleepless night, waking with the vision of him standing just outside our bedroom window the previous morning. I wondered if he knew it was the bedroom. Though we kept the shade drawn, and nobody could see in, I still had an uneasy feeling that some-thing lurked outside. It felt pretty similar to the way I could sense spirits nearby, though unseen. I called on my angels for protection and waited for morning.

Not seeing him when Lew picked me up in the morning, I began to wonder if the end of my ordeal was at hand. He did not appear in the parking lot at work, nor the bus stop as we drove past on the way home in the evening. Again Lew insisted on making sure I got into my apartment safely.

Several days passed without any contact or sightings of my stalker, so we began to let our guard down. Lew dropped me off without waiting again, and I resumed thinking I had learned a scary lesson about menacing strangers.

One evening about a week later, after Lew dropped me off, I realized that I had no groceries in the house. Elise would arrive home in time for dinner, and I wanted to cook something for the two of us. I hadn't seen my stalker, and figured that he had probably given up, so I decided to walk to the little market about a block away. I slung my shopping bag across my chest, dropped my wallet in the bottom, and headed out to do the shopping.

As I walked back home toward my house I saw someone sitting on the front steps with their face in their hands. I couldn't make out who, and thought that maybe one of the young men that rented the back apartment sat there enjoying the unseasonably pleasant night air.

As I got closer I realized that the man on the steps was my stalker. He hadn't noticed me, so I turned and quickly headed back to the market. I didn't know what I would do once there, but I knew I had to avoid him.

As I reached the market I saw my neighbors pull into the parking lot.

"Oh my GOD! I'm so glad you're here!" I exclaimed. "That obnoxious guy is creeping on the front step again!"

Elise and I had told them about my stalker and asked them to keep a lookout for him.

"We are grabbing a six pack, then heading home. Get in the car and we will go back together."

I climbed in the back seat, grateful for their protection, but terrified that my ordeal would continue, and perhaps escalate.

My neighbors parked on the side street and walked me to my front door. They both stood upwards of six feet tall and seemed extremely tough. They had grown up on the city streets and clearly would take no nonsense.

When he saw me walking up between two young men he jumped to his feet.

"What are you doing with *them?*" he screamed. "You need to be with *me*—only me. The Lord proclaimed it. You will be with me or with *nobody!*"

The implied violence in his sneer struck terror in my heart. I felt a real and present threat. I believed that he would easily kill me given a chance. He lunged toward us. One of the guys shoved him to the ground as I reflexively drew back. When he attempted to get up, quoting the Old Testament, my other protector set his six pack on the ground and grabbed my stalker by the shirt, pushing him down again.

"She doesn't belong to nobody, especially the likes of you! You've caused enough trouble for our friend here. It's time for us to take a ride."

My neighbors told me to put their beer in the fridge until they got back, then grabbed my stunned and babbling stalker by the arms dragging him to their car.

"What are you going to do?" I pleaded, "You're not going to hurt him are you?"

"No." one said, opening the car door to shove him in.

"Promise?" I begged, "Then what?"

"He's just going to have a long walk home," the other said, then they drove away.

After several hours Elise and I jumped as we heard a knock at the door. She opened it to find our grinning neighbors in the doorway.

"You didn't drink all our beer, did you?"

We invited them in for vegetable soup that I had kept hot on the stove.

"What did you do with him?" I worried that they had beaten him or worse. I knew that he posed a danger to me, but I also knew that he suffered from mental illness and didn't deserve a beating.

They told us that they didn't touch a hair on his head, but drove around the back roads in Mason and Livingston Counties for hours until they knew he didn't know where he was. Then they made him get out of the car in the middle of nowhere.

"He's gonna have a pretty long walk in the dark before he finds any place even to call someone." They laughed. "And if the cops pick him up, I'm sure they will take him to the psych ward!"

Though I did not want my stalker ever to bother me again, I felt thankful that the warm evening meant he would not freeze to death. Secretly, I hoped that the cops would take him to a place where he could get help, but I also hoped that his ordeal would deter him from continuing his pursuit of me.

After that scare, I became more cautious around strangers. Something had changed in how I perceived and approached the world. I noticed how men looked at me, tried to engage and possess me, always for their own purposes. I held back to avoid revealing my true self. I smiled and listened, but even that would prove ineffective in keeping me safe.

I began to turn more inward. I could not hear my guides. I felt abandoned by my angels. I just wanted to find a safe and quiet existence where I could live out whatever time the fates had allotted me.

One night I met an older man who treated me differently than any other I had met. At eighteen, thirty-two seemed so much older. He did not aggressively—or even coyly—attempt to gain access to my body. We talked about shared interests such as history and natural science. At parties where others drank and flirted, we played chess.

Elden invited me to Howell, where he lived, to meet his friends. He took me to dinner. We laughed and enjoyed each other's company.

I still attended parties at the house where several of Elise's friends lived. Though I had met my stalker there, he never showed up again.

Elise and I would hang out with our friends to watch weekly TV shows. They all felt like family. I felt safe in their company.

One week in the spring, Elise planned a backpacking trip with the folks who lived in the house where we watched TV. I, of course, could not backpack and so had to stay behind. All of the housemates except one planned to go on the trip. Since only two of us were left to fend for ourselves he offered to pick me up to go to Pitcher Night and listen to some live music. I agreed. At least on a peripheral level, we knew each other and had spent lots of time together watching TV or partying. The guys at that house felt like brothers to Elise and me, so I agreed.

After Paul picked me up, he told me that he had forgotten his wallet at home and had to stop there before heading to the bar. When I suggested I wait in the car, he insisted that I come inside.

"I have no idea where I left it, so it might take a while," he told me.

I agreed and followed him up the front porch steps. He unlocked and opened the door, motioning for me to enter ahead of him.

I smiled and walked into the darkened living room.

All at once, he was upon me. He spun me around and began kissing my mouth aggressively.

I pulled back, still in his grip.

"Stop it!" I insisted, "Stop it now!"

He ignored my pleas and pushed me backward onto the low sofa covered in brightly colored tapestries. I felt my knees buckle and wrench painfully.

"Ow!" I screamed, "Stop it, you are hurting me!"

Paul ignored my words and continued to grope my body, pulling at my clothes.

Unable to deter his assault, I let my body go limp. Silent tears rolled down my cheeks as he had his way.

When he finished, he got off me and sat on the sofa, smiling, as I awkwardly tried to tuck my clothes and spirit back in place.

I cannot accurately describe what I felt. I know that my body went numb. I felt flecks peel away from my spirit while my mind raced, trying to determine what I had done to cause him to misread my intention.

He apparently felt he had done nothing wrong.

"I'll go grab my wallet upstairs and be right down so we can go to *Lizards.*"

I felt so dirty and abused. Used. I determined that I must have done something to lead him on. I looked toward the front door, thinking that maybe I should just leave and walk home. My "date" had a car and could easily find me. He knew where I lived, and that I would be alone for the next ten days. I didn't move.

He came bouncing down the stairs.

"Found it!" He exclaimed happily, "Let's go."

He opened the front door, and I silently followed him to his car. I sat at a table in the bar with him as multiple people came up to greet him. One of his friends pulled up a chair between us and leered at me.

"What are you doing with this loser?" John joked. "You would do way better with me."

John looked me up and down, grinning hungrily.

I said nothing, but sat there smiling like a fool, as more shards of my spirit silently slipped away.

When the band finished, Paul suggested we leave. I wanted nothing more than to go home and take a long hot shower, but I did not know if he had other plans. I realized that I could not safely navigate the world as a young, unattached single woman.

"Yes," I said, smiling, "I'm exhausted and have to work in the morning. I'd like to go home."

We rode in silence until we reached my apartment. I quickly thought about how I would handle it if he asked to come inside.

"Thanks," he said grinning. "That was fun. I'll swing by from time to time. Maybe we should get back together while the cat's away ... if you know what I mean."

My face went ashen, and my stomach lurched. I knew exactly what he meant and yet still—minding my manners—I thanked him and said, "Sure."

As soon as I closed and locked my door, I began to tremble. He acted as if we both enjoyed his assault, and I did nothing to let him know otherwise.

After showering until the water ran cold, washing away all physical traces of him, I pulled on pajamas and climbed into bed. Though exhausted, sleep remained elusive.

The large bedroom window drew my eyes and thoughts towards it. I visualized my stalker lurking just outside. I thought about the events of the evening and pondered how someone I saw as a brother could completely misread or disregard my wishes. I felt extremely vulnerable and terrified.

Pulling the pillows and blankets off the bed, I made a pallet on the floor between the bed and the wall, hoping that anyone who forced their way in with ill intent would think the room empty. I curled up there and wept, longing for home.

When Elise returned, I told her that I had decided to move back home. I said that I had more doctor appointments, which was true, but I could've taken the train to appointments and returned the next day. We had no lease, but paid rent month to month, so my leaving would not leave her in the lurch. She could move in with other friends.

I gave my two-week notice at work, citing the same reasons for leaving. I never returned to watch TV at the place of my attack.

Elden drove me to the train, asking if he could write. I told him that I would like that. He kissed me gently and gave me a warm hug. Then I boarded the train for home.

I returned to the chaos and safety of my family, taking a job in the mail room at the company where my mother worked. I simply existed. My wounded spirit did not travel. I did not meditate, nor seek further enlightenment. I only sought safety. Had I believed in the doctrine, I might have considered a religious life, but I had nothing. My spirit fluttered like shredded sails that set me adrift for many years.

Elden wrote beautiful letters laced with poetry. He rode the train to visit a few times, then encouraged me to move to Howell to live closer to him. My house was full to bursting with little ones. I felt safe with Elden. I was no longer available to whoever might decide I was something expendable to be used and discarded at will. I agreed.

I packed my belongings and moved into an apartment above a law office across the street from the Livingston County Courthouse. I applied at the local hospital and was hired. Elden lived with his parents, but spent more and more time with me. He introduced me to his coworkers and friends. I settled into an uneventful life. One day his mother asked out of the blue when we planned to get married.

Elden replied, "June."

Though that was the first I heard of it, I smiled sheepishly and accepted his mother's hugs and celebration.

We married in June at my family's lake in Wisconsin.

⁕⁙⁚⁚⁙⁖

Elden quickly grew cold and unavailable. If I tried to converse, he would look up from his book, glare at me, saying, "You can see that I am busy."

He asked me to only play my dulcimer, or sing when he worked since my voice "hurt his ears." I complied. I stopped trying. I stopped feeling. I stopped being. I focused on my hospital job delivering records and samples on a little cart. I saved my money. I had acquaintances with whom I grew friendly. We played music together and had bonfires and parties. I got to know Laura who was married to Elden's coworker and friend, Doug. We had coffee in her kitchen as I played with her young children.

Evenings, I walked the streets of Howell, frequently finding myself at a beautiful cemetery by the lake. I often ended up at the same graveside where a sizeable stone was inscribed, *Preston*. In its shadow rested several smaller grave markers, including those of twin baby girls, *Birdie Rae* and *Hattie Mae*. I felt somehow connected to them, but I did not know how or why.

Dad mailed me books and articles in an attempt to pull me out of my stifling small-town consciousness. When I contemplated attending the university, Elden said I would never pass the entrance exams. Dad told me to schedule the test and give it my best.

Elden worked nights. He got home before seven each morning, which gave me ample time to take our only car and drive to Michigan State for the entrance exam. On the day of my exam, I got up, dressed, and waited by the door for his return, watching the clock tick away the minutes.

He did not return until well after eight, which meant I could not make the scheduled exam. He apologized profusely.

"A delivery truck pulled in just as we were ready to punch out. Doug and I had to stay to unload it." Disappointed! Accustomed to disappointment by this time, I said nothing as he lumbered toward his solitary bedroom to sleep the day away.

Later that morning, I ran into Laura, Doug's wife, in the grocery store.

"What a sweet thing Elden did this morning, treating Doug to breakfast at *The Clock*."

"What?" I asked.

"Yeah," She said, "He told Doug that he wanted to go out for breakfast and invited him along. What a great boss!"

I grew livid. Not only had Elden thwarted my chance to take the exam, but he had lied about it. I could not fathom why he would try to sabotage me. He had told me that I would fail. Maybe he wanted to save me from that. What I did know was that I would not let it happen again.

When I returned home, I contacted the university to find out if I could schedule the exam at another time. I signed up for the following week, saying nothing to Elden. On the day of the exam, I set my alarm to go off before he came home. While the house was quiet, I got up, dressed, and climbed back in bed until I heard him close the door to his bedroom and turn on the fan. Then I slipped downstairs, grabbed the keys, and drove to East Lansing, returning before he woke up looking for a meal before going to work.

Two weeks later, I received my acceptance letter from MSU. Not only did they admit me, but they waved most of my freshman classes.

"Wow." He said when I showed him the letter. "I thought you missed the exam."

"I rescheduled," I replied, smiling gleefully as I turned to walk away.

CHAPTER 15: VISION

['vi-zhən] *noun*, a supernatural appearance that conveys a revelation.

ONE DEEP WINTER EVENING, my friend Laura and I drove to visit her older sister who lived just over an hour away. We laughed and talked for hours until we noticed the weather had taken a turn for the worse. The wind began to blow, and snow fell heavily.

We said our good-byes, and set out for home. Laura drove. Anxiety grew as visibility deteriorated into whiteout conditions. Unable to see beyond a few feet, we commented on how grateful we were to have most of our journey involve a four-lane divided highway. Laura switched on her flashers to make sure that any truck or car moving at a faster speed than our nervous crawl would see us and slow down before hitting us from behind.

My eyes strained to help keep us from inadvertently sliding into the ditch. Not a single track appeared on the road in front of us.

"For all I know, we could be in the middle of a field!" Laura laughed, attempting to break the tension.

"Keep your eyes peeled," she instructed, "I don't want to miss our exit. I can't see a thing up ahead."

"Got it," I replied, straining my eyes to catch a road sign indicating our location or exit.

Suddenly, in the distance, I noticed bright lights heading swiftly toward us. By the height and intensity, I assumed they belonged to a semi on the other side of the highway. Though still in the distance, it soon became apparent that the headlights continued directly toward us at a high rate of speed.

"What's that?" I asked.

"What?" Said Laura turning to glance at me in the passenger seat.

The lights increased in intensity and speed. Impact seemed inevitable.

"LOOK OUT!" I screamed, bracing for a deadly impact.

Laura jerked her attention back to the road. In an instant, the light whooshed past and through me. As it reached me, I clearly saw the illuminated face of Grammie Ethel smiling at me. As the vision impacted, she turned her head, fixing her smiling gaze on me as "she" passed by and disappeared.

"Holy shit!" I exclaimed.

"What was that about?" Said Laura, "You're freaking me out."

"Sorry," I replied, shaken, "I thought I saw something."

At long last, we found our exit and made our way through the abandoned, snow-covered streets to my door. Thanking Laura and reminding her to drive carefully the rest of the way to her house, I climbed the stairs to my apartment, still feeling the powerful presence of Grammie Ethel.

Grammie had suffered for decades with rheumatoid arthritis. Her body had begun to shut down from the wreckage. I knew how much she suffered, and I had actively prayed for release and relief. Grammie Ethel and I shared a special secret. She had revealed to me that she, too, spirit-traveled. I assumed that what I had seen was her out for a fly-about making sure I returned home safely. I pulled out a pad of paper, pencil, and my dulcimer and began writing a song for her:

Grandma's Song

Look in her eyes and you'll see the blue waters,
They're deep as the ocean, and wide as the skies.
Her love reaches distances I'll never travel,

A love I knew deep in those ocean blue eyes.

Grandma, Oh, Grandma
I love you so dearly.
Just knowing you has helped me in so many ways.
Grandma, Oh, Grandma,
I see you quite clearly,
Your strength will inspire me all of my days.

Though Life's full of sadness she keeps bringing joy to us,
Laughter and smiles fill most of our time.
And when I feel burdened by everyday sorrows,
I think of you, Grandma, and love fills my mind.

Grandma, Oh, Grandma,
I love you so dearly.
Just knowing you has helped me in so many ways.
Grandma, Oh, Grandma,
I see you quite clearly,
Your strength will inspire me all of my days.

Just as I erased and touched up the last edits, the loud ring of my telephone startled me. Looking at the clock, I realized the late hour and jumped to answer.

"H-hello?" I stammered, trembling from shock and dread.

"Tiyi, it's Mom... I wanted to let you know that Grammie Ethel died tonight."

Speechless, I glanced over at my newly finished song.

"Are you alright?" Mom asked "Did you hear me?"

"Yes. Sorry. Okay. What time did she die?" I asked

When she told me the time, I realized that she died at almost the exact moment I saw her fly by in a vision of light.

"Are you doing okay, Mom?" I asked.

"I'm just fine," she replied. "Grammie Ethel will never have to suffer again. It's a really good thing. She was ready."

"I love you, Mom."

"I love you too, darlin'. I'll let you know when we have funeral arrangements in place."

"Okay, Mom. I'll be there for sure.

After hanging up, I returned to my song. With tears falling, I sang it, start to finish, for the first time. Then I had a good cry and went to bed.

Lying there, I began to feel guilty that I had prayed for her death. I felt confused and filled with grief and remorse. These feelings followed me for several days.

The night before I planned to travel home for Grammie Ethel's funeral, I experienced a powerful dream.

Walking into Grammie Ethel's room in the nursing home where she had lived for several years, I found her sitting upright in bed.

"There you are!" She said with a conspiratorial smile and a sly wink.

"Grammie..." I began.

"I've been waiting for you." She continued.

Then she reached down to grab the top of the blanket that covered her. I immediately noticed that her once-gnarled and useless hands appeared smooth and perfect. She saw me looking at them, laughed, then threw the covers off herself, swinging her perfect legs over the side of the bed.

"You thought you could kill me." She smiled cunningly. "Ha!"

To my surprise, she leapt from the bed and stood perfectly straight with no support. I stood a few feet away, aghast, taking it all in. Then she began to lean toward me, still grinning widely. Next, she turned to look at the open window, then shot in a flash through it, disappearing into the blue sky.

I awoke with a start, tears streaming down my face.

"Thank you, Grammie!" I said to the empty room. "I love you. Fly away."

Chapter 16: Deliverance

[di-'li-v(ə-)rən(t)s] *noun*, the act of delivering someone or something.

REALIZING THAT ONE CAR WOULD NOT SUFFICE for our conflicting schedules as I attended the university while Elden worked nights at The A&P, we bought a compact car for me to drive back and forth to school. The car, and my emerging confidence, brought new levels of independence I had never experienced before.

I loved attending classes at MSU. I absorbed every bit of knowledge, making connections to things I already knew plus exploring wonders I didn't even realize I wanted to know. Completely immersing myself in my studies provided respite from the emptiness I felt in my life in Howell. My advisor waived several of my classes due to my score on the entrance exam, but also because the buildings in which they took place were inaccessible to me.

Elise lived in East Lansing, though we seldom talked. She had her life among her friends, and I had mine among my husband's. One late spring afternoon, Elise invited me to attend a backyard party. Elden did not want to attend, so I decided to go alone. I knew I would be among strangers, so I decided to bring my dulcimer. Playing an instrument helped to eliminate awkward small talk.

Shortly after I arrived, Elise spotted me and introduced me to her boyfriend, Scott, a smiling, red-haired, boisterous, and bearded fellow. I liked him right away.

"There's someone else I want you to meet," said Elise as she disappeared into the house. I continued to play until she returned.

"This is David, Scott's brother."

Looking into the biggest, darkest, brown eyes I had ever seen, I introduced myself.

"You two should know each other," she announced as a matter-of-fact and left us alone in the room.

David smiled and sat down near me. He seemed strangely familiar. Though impossible, it felt as if I had known him many times before. I resisted a strong urge to put my arms around him and ask where he had been. Instead, we began to talk.

We talked for hours as our connection kindled, or perhaps rekindled. I learned that David had recently returned from Thailand, where he served in the Peace Corps. He returned with a Thai wife. I told him about Elden, Howell, and growing up in Chicago. He told me about growing up in North India. We spoke about music and musicians, and all the most essential interests I had locked away during the years I'd spent in Howell. I played a Donovan song that I had learned on the dulcimer. He listened, gazing at my face as I sang, which made my heart leap in my chest. Then he closed his eyes and told me that it was beautiful.

I wondered: *How is it possible that two people born half a world apart, living completely different lives, with different experiences, had somehow found each other—again, in this lifetime?*

We spoke about dreams for the future and a world we each wanted to help create. We talked for hours until it became apparent the party had ended, and we, alone, remained.

"I should go." I said, rising stiffly from my chair, "I've got a long drive home in the dark."

"Okay." He replied, rising with me. "I'll walk you to your car."

Closing the car door, he added, "Go well. Stay well."

Butterflies danced in my belly, and my heart pounded as I said, "You as well," and drove off toward the highway, back to a life where some other girl lived, not the real me now struggling to resurface.

After that David and I had no contact. I continued to commute to MSU from Howell and back, always returning to an empty house. Months later, Elise asked me to meet her at a bar for some "girl time." She and Scott had a falling out, and she wanted to talk.

"He never wants to stay at my house. I always have to go there if we want to sleep together. It drives me crazy!" She complained.

"Well, did you ask him why?" I inquired.

"He says he's more comfortable at his place. He doesn't like the cat or dogs on the bed."

"I can relate." I laughed.

"We haven't seen each other in a couple of days." She went on.

"Sounds like you both are just being stubborn."

"Yeah, you're probably right. Let's go over there to see him. I bet David would be happy to see *you* too, especially since his wife split. He and Scott share a house, you know." She smirked.

My face flushed. Looking away, hoping Elise wouldn't notice, I agreed to accompany her.

We found Scott and David in the basement of their house on Foster Street, watching *On The Road with Charles Kuralt* on a TV in the corner. The pungent aroma of marijuana filled the air.

Elise descended the basement stairs before me,

"Who's there?" Scott asked.

"It's us," replied Elise as she leaned down so he could see her in the partially-open staircase.

I followed close behind, placing my cane carefully to navigate the steep stairs.

"Who's that with the cane?" David asked.

As I made my way cautiously down the basement stairs, I watched David's face flush. He raised his eyebrows in sheer delight, clearly overjoyed to see me.

"Oh wow!" He exclaimed, jumping to his feet. "It's you!"

Though we had only met once before and hadn't seen each other in months, it felt as if no time had passed. David made room for me to sit next to him, as Scott handed Elise a joint. We spoke few words, and I only stayed about an hour, but in that short time I felt our souls further entwine.

Later that summer, my younger siblings rode the train to Michigan for an adventure. We planned a campout on some property that Elden had bought for hunting. Elden's friends from Howell joined us for the afternoon. Since she knew my siblings from our teen years, I invited Elise, along with Scott and his other roommates—David included—to join us. Most of us camped out under the stars, except for Elden, who wanted to sleep in his bed, along with his friends who lived nearby and decided to return to their beds too.

That night, after everyone else had fallen asleep, cozily tucked into sleeping bags scattered near the fire, David and I continued to talk in soft voices. We had positioned our sleeping bags next to one another. Stars shone in the night sky even though the full moon cast bright light in the void. We talked about the future. I had no idea what lay in store for me, nor even how long I would have, but I knew that whatever time I had in this life I wanted it to include this beautiful, kind, and loving man.

After a long silence listening to only the crackling of the fire as it turned to embers, David leaned close and, ever so gently, touched his lips to mine. Neither of us moved. I barely breathed, but I felt as if I breathed in his very soul, exhaling mine into him. It lasted forever and was far too brief, as we simultaneously noticed a strange phenomenon in the night sky.

It appeared as if delicate streams of light fell from the stars, dissipating just above our heads. The air felt charged and electric.

"What *is* that?" He said, sitting up.

"Wow," I responded in awe, also sitting up.

We both gazed in amazement at this incredible shower of soft, shimmering light. Then I noticed what looked like a path illuminated by moonlight across the alfalfa field.

"Look, a path. Should we follow it?" I asked with excitement.

We had been talking for hours about finding our paths with heart. Then suddenly, an illuminated path appeared before us.

"Of course." He said, helping me up. "Maybe it's our path."

As we walked, arm in arm following the moonlight, the universe continued to rain wavy streams of light down on us. I felt as if in a dream, memory, or a separate reality. I knew I had taken this journey sometime long ago, with the person beside me.

Across the field, where we could no longer see the fire, we stopped, faced each other, and embraced. I could feel his warmth, and his heartbeat as everything else in the world faded into that one pivotal moment.

Then, without warning, the night began to feel chilly and damp. I noticed heavy dew on the alfalfa, though it had been dry moments before. The light shower and path had disappeared. I am not sure what reality we had just experienced, but now we somehow found ourselves back in ordinary reality. David helped me as we made our way back to the fire, which, to my surprise, burned only about twenty feet away.

Though I would not see him again for several months, my life had found a new path. I had no idea how it would come to fruition, but I intended to follow it wherever it led.

I continued focusing on my studies and my life in East Lansing, spending less and less time in Howell. Elden's and my paths seldom crossed. I often remarked that the only way I knew he still lived there was evident in the shrinking peanut butter in the jar.

I began to spend more time with Elise and the people who lived on Foster Street in the house with Scott and David. I immersed myself in the blossoming music scene in East Lansing, connecting to many great friends, and volunteering as press coordinator for The Ten Pound Fiddle, a folk society at MSU. This exposed me to even more music and musicians.

We would sit in the Foster Street living room and play music for hours. Here my voice did not hurt anyone's ears, nor did it in the other jam sessions or song circles in which we participated. I began to feel happy, accepted, and loved.

My right knee continued to deteriorate, causing greater and greater pain. I found it difficult to walk even using a cane, sometimes two canes.

Mom made an appointment for me with my surgeon in Chicago. He determined that I needed more surgery to keep me walking. I agreed and scheduled it immediately after spring classes ended.

Elden told me that he wanted to save his vacation time for hunting season, so I took the train alone to Chicago. Mom and everybody else in my family had gone Up North for the 4th of July, leaving only Dad in Chicago to work. He sent his assistant to pick me up at Union Station.

"Where's your husband?" She asked incredulously, as she picked up my small bag.

"He had to work," I said. "Will you drive me to the hospital? I have to check in this afternoon for all my pre-surgery stuff."

"Does your dad know you're here alone?" She asked.

"No," I replied. "I don't think so."

I had grown so used to the lack of interest Elden showed toward me, and his disengaged absence of support, that her indignity surprised me.

"I'll be okay," I said, smiling sheepishly, "It's not like I haven't been through this before."

"That's just crazy!" She exclaimed. "I'm calling your father as soon as we get to the hospital to tell him I'm staying with you today. This is just not acceptable."

"It's okay … really," I pleaded, "It will just be a lot of sitting around."

"Too bad," she stated. "I'm not leaving you to go through this alone."

She sat with me in X-ray, the lab, admission, and accompanied me to my room before leaving. That night Dad came after work and paced nervously in my semi-private room. He told me that he needed to prepare for an upcoming trial but would be there in the morning before I went in for surgery. He told me he would stay there until I got back to my room.

Dad lovingly gathered a clump of my hair on the top of my head in his fingers, and lifted it with his signature *"bloop,"* then kissed me on my head.

"See you bright and early." He said with a lame attempt to appear cheerful.

Since nobody occupied the bed next to me, I sat up in my bed feeling completely alone. Though I didn't feel frightened about the surgery, I did feel anxious for the pain I knew lay ahead during my recovery. My thumbs ached with loneliness. I picked up the phone and called one of my best buddies from childhood, Moose.

"Hi. Guess where I am?" I said.

"Are you at your folk's?" He asked, elated.

"Nope, even closer. I'm at Saint Francis, having more surgery tomorrow."

Moose studied at Northwestern University. He minored in medicine and majored in neuropharmacology. He studied and worked all the time, but Saint Francis Hospital was only blocks away from where he lived.

"I'll be right over," he said, "Don't go anywhere."

We both laughed at the absurdity of that statement.

Moose came to sit with me, holding my hand for hours. We laughed and told stupid jokes.

A nurse came in and said, "Visiting hours are over."

Then she smiled and closed the door leaving us alone.

After another hour, Moose said, "I really should go. I have work in the lab that I need to finish tonight. I'll see you tomorrow after you've gone under the knife."

"Right," I said with a huff, "Can't wait."

He squeezed my hand and left, turning at the door to smile lovingly.

I refused sleep medication when the nurse offered it. I planned to spirit-travel away from the hospital that night, and I did not want anything fogging up my brain. As I lay on the bed, absolutely still, focusing on my breath and the space between my eyebrows, I called on my angels and guides to stand beside me. So much time had passed since I had reached out to them that I wasn't sure they would hear me.

I watched as colored light swirled within my inner vision. Yellow faded to amber, that faded to green, then blue, red, and finally the deepest indigo. I noticed twisted faces in my periphery attempting to obstruct my journey. Soon I saw the pinprick of white light far in the distance. Ignoring the terrifying faces at the edges, I focused my complete attention on that light. I felt a sensation of flying swiftly through a vast tunnel. The whooshing sound that I heard initially began to develop form and cadence as if the universe itself was singing.

The white light grew as I passed through an undulating tunnel. All at once I felt myself shoot, at great speed, into the white light entirely, then outward and up. Up beyond the city, beyond the clouds, beyond the full moon and the heavens, I soared upward beyond any distance I had ever traveled, then slowed my consciousness to float in the blackness of space.

At this distance, I could not feel my body. I also experienced a total absence of sound—no beating heart—no sound of my breath—even my thoughts existed in profound silence. This was a complete void. I felt so incredibly peaceful, almost euphoric. I experienced nothingness, and it pleased me.

Before long, however, I heard the sound of Grammie Ethel far in the distance. She called my name.

"Come home!" She called. "Come home."

I felt my spirit drop rapidly until I could again hear the sound of my heart, then I awoke with a gasp and a start. Dad stood by my bed, alongside a nurse and orderly.

"Are you ready?" The nurse asked. "It's time to go."

Startled wide awake, I rubbed my eyes and nodded.

"Your mother and I will say a novena while you are in the operating room. Everything will be just fine.' He said, to calm and convince himself as much as me. I, on the other hand, had no fear at all. I had reconnected with the safest place to wait out the ordeal ahead.

⁕⁚⁖⁙⁚⁖

I awoke in terrible pain. My heel felt as if it was on fire. My back and shoulders throbbed, and piercing pain radiated from hip to toe in my right leg. "Open your eyes," the nurse demanded.

"No." I refused, "I don't want to stay here."

I began to cry.

"She's in agony!" My father screamed, "Give her something for the love of God!"

"It's just the anesthesia." The nurse said condescendingly.

Dad was having none of this. "Jesus Christ!" He screamed, "Give her something for the pain, or call the doctor immediately! I am NOT asking!"

Moments later, morphine dripped into my body through the IV in my hand. Pain evolved into wild hallucinations, or perhaps visions. I saw gray figures standing around the room staring at me. None tried to communicate, thank goodness, because I could not control this state of consciousness. I felt woozy, my head spinning. When I tried to remove my spirit from my wracked body, I saw Grammie Ethel standing in front of me, shaking her head, "No". Relinquishing control, I drifted into unconsciousness.

I vaguely recall several attendants at my bedside throughout the night. A team of nurses frequently changed my bandages. I remember my doctor at my bed side expressing concern because my incision would not stop bleeding. As the doctor packed clean dressings into the open wound on my leg, I screamed in agony. Again I tried to leave my body, but Grammie Ethel blocked my way.

"Not now," She said firmly. "You can't leave now. You have to stop bleeding."

In my delirium, I saw her reach out and place her hand on my bleeding wound. Suddenly I recognized my allies. The white and amber spirits stood at my sides. I felt warmth and peace emanating from their forms. The indigo ally reached down and replaced Grammie Ethel's hands as she faded away. Then I fell into welcome unconsciousness.

I don't know how long I remained in that state, but when I came to, flowers filled my room, and Moose sat next to my bed stroking my hair. The pain had turned into pressure. I saw that my leg had been immobilized in a box with thick, bulging bandages.

"There you are." Said Moose. "Do you need anything?"

I indicated that I needed water. He held the straw to my lips, and I took a long drink from the ice water. Then I tried to sit up on my elbows.

"No, no no." Moose said, gently pushing my shoulders back. "You can't sit up yet. Your body kept leaking. You really scared us."

"What do you mean *leaking?*" I asked, confused.

"Bleeding," he clarified. "Your incision bled a lot!"

"Full moon," I said, recalling the moon I'd seen while traveling the night before surgery.

I did not protest but relaxed on my pillow, weak and confused.

"You're okay now," he said. "You've got a good team here."

I stayed flat on my back for days while my incision slowly began to heal. Moose and Dad visited every day. Dad stayed a few minutes. Moose stayed hours. Elden never called. His mother, Lela called after several days to see how I was getting along. Mom called from Up North, and I got calls from David and the Foster Street crew nearly every day.

After several days a package arrived from Lansing. It contained notes from all of my Foster Street friends and cassette tapes they had made while sitting in the living room playing music. They spoke to me as if I was there. David stated several times that they could hear my voice in harmony on the songs. The tapes filled me with joy. I missed them and knew how much they loved me. At the bottom of the package, I found a small cardboard matchbox labeled Magic Beans. It held several dried black turtle beans with a tiny note stating: "Magic Beans to use any way you choose, signed with David's name in Hindi.

After two weeks without hearing a word from him, I got a call from Elden. He told me that he was coming to visit on the weekend. He'd only be able to see me for a short time because he had to get back in time to sleep before work.

Listening to him made my thumbs ache, my spirit shrink, and my heart break even more. He made it very clear that visiting me created an imposition. I figured that his mother had forced him to come. She had

no idea that I did not want or need to see him. I had emotionally separated from Elden almost entirely by this time.

That Saturday, he walked into my hospital room with an uncomfortable crooked grin on his face and a brown paper bag in his hands.

"Hi Cutes." He said as he crossed the room.

I mistakenly thought that he had brought me a gift in that brown
bag, but instead he pulled the curtain closed between my roommate and
us, turned the chair to face the TV, sat down, and pulled a six-pack of
Hamm's beer from the bag.

"You get WGN on this thing, right?" He asked, picking up the
remote.

Then he found the channel and sat there watching an old cowboy
movie, silently drinking his beer. He didn't ask how I felt. He never asked
about my progress or prognosis. He said absolutely nothing until the
movie ended.

I remained in my bed, fuming silently.

Why bother? I thought, *if I try to say anything he will just say that I can
see that he's busy.*

When the movie ended, at last, he stood and placed the empties in
the bag with his other beers.

"Well," he said, not making eye contact, "I've got to get back to your
dad's to catch the early train tomorrow. G'bye, Cutes."

Then he left. Just like that! Instantly my roommate flung back the
dividing curtain.

"Who the Hell was that?!" she demanded.

We had shared the room for more than a week. She had suffered
whiplash from an auto accident. Every morning she did her full makeup
and dressed in fancy negligees with matching slippers. She had dyed her
hair red. I pictured her in some corner bar in the city. She spoke tough
and told the truth. We had become convenient friends.

"That's my husband," I answered.

"*THAT'S* your husband? Well then, who's that other guy who is up
in here every single night?"

"That's my pal, Moose," I explained.

"Boy!" she said, shaking her head dramatically, "Did you ever marry the wrong guy!"

"Boy," I repeated. *"Did I ever* marry the wrong guy."

Several days later, the doctor scheduled me for physical therapy. I would be able to get out of bed at long last, into a wheelchair, and out of that tiny room for a most welcome change of scenery.

My first excursion was thwarted when I became woozy and felt faint as the nurses helped me upright toward the wheelchair. I had to wait a few hours until I felt more stable, then wait for therapy the next day. Later, after my head felt cleared, the nurses helped me into the wheelchair after all.

That evening, Moose wheeled me through the halls of the hospital and out into a lovely courtyard where I could breathe fresh air and smell Lake Michigan. I longed to have this ordeal behind me. I longed to have so very much behind me.

The next day at physical therapy, I had to lay on a large cushioned table in the middle of a room filled with staff and other patients while my therapist lifted and rotated my painfully stiff atrophied leg. I felt self-conscious in my hospital gown with only a towel between my legs.

Next, I had to turn over onto my belly. The seemingly basic maneuver proved extremely difficult and painful. Once I assumed that position, the therapist began other stretching exercises that shot terrible pain through my body.

"Only ten more," he said as I began to cry.

Looking up through my tears, I saw several people staring at me with pity in their eyes. I squeezed my own eyes tightly to try to shut them out, but more to stop crying. I felt weak and humiliated having to endure torture in public.

Back in my room, I felt utterly exhausted and defeated. The phone rang. To my surprise, I heard Elden's voice. I shouldn't have said anything, but I had just been through such a terrible ordeal and I had to tell someone. I told him about the difficult procedures, and how I broke down right in front of everybody in the room.

"Jesus!" he said tersely, "You always panic!"

Now I felt not only humiliated but admonished. I said nothing else. After a minute, his mother came on the line. Now it made sense. She had made him call me from her house. When she asked how I felt, I simply told her "Fine."

Hanging up after only a couple of minutes, I swallowed hard to keep the lump in my throat from turning into a sob. I didn't want to "panic" again.

The phone rang. I picked it up and this time heard David on the other end. The sound of his voice soothed and comforted me.

He asked me about therapy. I told him what had happened. I explained that Elden told me I always panic when I told him that I had cried.

"You ... NEVER ... panic." David spoke sincerely, "You are the bravest, strongest woman I know. You are the bravest, strongest human I have *ever* known. Elden hasn't a clue who you really are."

I believed him. Tears fell down my face as I listened to the love and concern in his voice.

"Everyone here who knows you realizes that you are amazing. We all love you ... I love you."

More tears fell. *Boy! Did I marry the wrong guy!*

In another week, I was ready for discharge. I needed to get to the airport to fly to Duluth to recover at the lake Up North with Mom instead of being isolated in Howell. Dad had a trial, and Moose didn't have a car, so Elden was forced to drive to Chicago to help me on my way.

He arrived the day before my discharge.

"We have to talk.' I told him.

"Not here," he replied, sensing the seriousness in my voice and gesturing to my roommate in the other bed.

"Wheel me downstairs. There's a courtyard where we can sit."

I will never forget the look my roommate flashed as we left. She knew what I intended to discuss. I saw her disapproval of Elden mixed in with encouragement for me to stand up to him. I smiled and nodded as Elden, oblivious, pushed me through the door.

He sat on a bench. I sat in the wheelchair facing him. He smiled awkwardly, clearly uncomfortable.

"I want a divorce," I finally said flatly.

"Okay," he said, looking down at his hands.

We sat in silence for several minutes.

"Don't you want to know why?" I asked incredulously. "Don't you want to talk about it?"

He looked at me without emotion, "I'm sure you have your reasons."

That was all. We never discussed it further, ever.

After four weeks in the hospital and several more recuperating Up North, I returned to Howell, contacted the Women's Law Clinic in Lansing, and began divorce proceedings.

I remained in close contact with David and my Foster Street friends as the legal wheels turned, and Elden went on with his daily routine as if nothing had changed. For me, however, everything had changed.

One weekend, David told me that he was meeting several college friends in Ann Arbor for the art fair. He wanted me to join him to meet them.

So that Saturday, Elden invited his friends, Doug and Laura, to join us for a day at the Art Fair.

We loaded up my wheelchair and set out to meet up with David and his friends. After only a couple of hours, Elden announced that they wanted to get back. He said we had to leave.

I did not want to leave after only experiencing a small part of the fair's music and amazing exhibits. David offered to look out for me. He planned to stay with several friends at Douglass and Patricia's apartment in Ann Arbor. I did not ask if I could stay. I told Elden that I was staying, and David would bring me home on Sunday.

While Doug and Laura shot shocked glances in his direction, Elden had no choice but to agree. I sat in my chair, watching my life in Howell disappear down the crowded street, then David grabbed the handles of my chair, and we went rolling gleefully in the other direction.

That day I not only met more of David's friends from Albion College, but many musicians who became lifelong friends. David navigated my wheelchair through the crowded streets of the city as we laughed and talked.

Sitting in a wheelchair means that conversations mostly happen over your head as folks stand around your chair. Though it's not intentional, it would still leave me feeling left out to a certain extent, and uncomfortable having to crane my neck to look up. David, on the other hand, would always squat down next to my chair to bring the conversation to me. He wore a Sikh bangle on his arm. I recall how it felt as he lifted my arm to place on his. I fell deeper in love every minute, with every touch.

That night at his friend's apartment in Ann Arbor, Douglas and Patricia gave us their room so I could sleep more comfortably in a bed while everyone else found couches or places on the floor. We lay side by side so close that no space remained between us. He leaned in and kissed me long and gently on my lips. I remembered the last and only time our lips had touched as electricity rushed through every cell in my body. As the kisses became deeper and passion grew, I protested. "I can't." I said,

"It's okay." He replied, "I understand."

I wanted more than anything to let our bodies throw off all care and come together in ecstasy, but knew that this could not be the time. I also knew the time would come.

The next day we took the bus into the city to the art fair. In the late 1970s, accessible public transit did not yet exist, but that did not stop us. When the bus stopped, Douglas and David lifted me out of the chair and carried me onto the bus while others collapsed the chair and brought it aboard.

They made it so much fun that I did not feel self-conscious in the least. I did not feel like a burden or an inconvenience. I felt like part of a great adventure.

When we arrived at the Quad at U of M, David wheeled my chair to the center, and climbed up on a ledge. He threw his arms wide and spoke to the crowd.

"*I LOVE THIS WOMAN!*"

He shouted to the cheers and applause of our friends and bystanders.

Then he leapt down and kissed me right there in front of the whole world.

"I love you too," I said with tears welling in my eyes. "I do love you too."

CHAPTER 17: INCIPIENCE

[in-'si-pē-ən(t)s] *noun*, Beginning

DAVID AND I SPENT MORE AND MORE TIME TOGETHER as our deep connection and love grew. In early November I began to feel ill and exhausted so I made an appointment with my doctor. I was pregnant. That night, David and I attended an album naming party for our friend Sally Rogers. A pint of good Irish whiskey served as an incentive for whoever came up with the best name. The album was later named *The Unclaimed Pint.*

David told me that a former Peace Corp friend had contacted him, begging him to join her in Thailand to help process the influx of Indo-chinese refugees flooding over the border as the Khmer Rouge began its bloody purge following the Việt Nam War. He struggled over the deci-sion to stay or go.

He had served in Thailand for several years, and he spoke the language fluently. His services seemed essential to help countless desperate people seeking refuge from slaughter. Reluctant to make my pregnancy a deciding factor or to have it keep him from the best use of his gifts, I decided not to tell him about the baby until after he had made his decision. Still, I continued moving forward with my divorce from Elden.

That Christmas, Elden and I went to Chicago to spend time with my family. He hadn't accompanied me on a visit for over a year, telling me that he did not like my family, especially my mother.

As folks commented that it was nice to see him I replied flippantly,

"Well, it's probably the last time you will see him, so don't get used to it."

Confused, they'd laugh awkwardly.

I never came right out to declare that Elden and I were divorcing. Nobody in my family had ever done that, and I just didn't want to risk any fallout at that moment. Elden had succeeded in isolating me from my family. I had stopped speaking of anything personal with anyone. Elden had succeeded in making me feel like a ghost among those who loved me most.

Everyone gathered in the living room, talking and laughing boisterously. Elden, obviously uncomfortable, sat silently in a wingback chair wearing an awkward grin when the phone rang.

"It's for you." My little brother declared, handing me the receiver.

Surprised, I put it to my ear and put my finger in the other in order to hear whomever waited on the other end.

"Hello?"

"Why didn't you tell me we are having a baby?"

David waited for my response. I hadn't told a single soul. How did he know? People ignored my phone call as the living room erupted in a raucous burst of laughter.

"Hold on." I said shakily, " Let me get to a different extension. I can't hear myself think in here."

Handing the phone to my sister, I instructed her to hang up when I got to the phone upstairs.

"Who is it?" She asked.

"Just a friend. I can't hear with all this going on down here."

I waited anxiously for a few seconds, staring at the phone on the wall in the hallway upstairs. When I picked it up, I listened to the loud chatter of my family in the room downstairs. Next, I slid down the wall to sit on the floor below the wall-mounted phone.

"Okay, I've got it. You can hang up now, thanks."

I heard a click, then silence from the extension.

"Hello." David repeated, "When did you plan to tell me?"

He sounded hurt. "I ... I don't know. I didn't want it to sway your decision about the refugee camps."

"I could never go." I heard his voice crack as he swallowed a sob. "Every time I pictured leaving you, it broke my heart. I've been crying for days. Now, are we going to have a baby?"

"Yes," I replied. "How did you know? Nobody knows but me. How?"

"I dreamt it last night. I couldn't wait until you got back to find out, so I called. I got the number from Elise."

"What did you dream?" I asked.

"I dreamed that you were sitting on a riverbank making a daisy crown. You set it on your head, then made another tiny one. Then you said, 'This one is for our daughter.' I knew immediately that we would have a daughter. I'm never going anywhere too far from you or our daughter. You can count on that."

"Okay," I said with tears in my eyes, "but what about Thailand?"

"Somebody else can do that. I could never leave you. I will never leave you."

With hearts bursting, we bid goodbye, making plans to meet as soon as I returned from Chicago. Though I wanted to tell everyone about my pending divorce, as well as the growing baby in my belly, I decided it needed to wait. Everyone would assume that Elden had fathered the baby, though, in truth, it was impossible. We hadn't touched one another in over a year. He had checked out, then I did. I didn't want to think about how I would explain the intricacies of my waning life with Elden and the emergence of my new life, one in which—side by side with my love—I would raise a family and find my true path with heart.

When I told Elden about my pregnancy, he pragmatically asked how I intended to pay for it. All my savings were earmarked for college. I needed to finish my degree to get my teaching certificate in order to support myself and my child. I hadn't thought it all through. His insurance would cover all my medical needs as long as we were married. If I left, insurance would not cover my expenses. I felt inadequate and foolish. Elden had a way of making me feel small and incompetent, masterfully using my insecurities to control me.

"I don't know. " I replied. "I just know that I cannot stay here."

"You know," he said, looking down, "I will never get married again. It's just not for me. I hate being married."

I felt a lump in my throat. What had I done that made him so miserable. He hated everything about our years together. From the very beginning he made it perfectly clear that any need for comfort or support reflected a flaw. In his eyes, my physical and emotional needs made me weak. I felt insignificant and vulnerable.

"My mother probably won't ever have a grandchild."

He knew that I loved his mother. She had a generous heart and treated me with kindness and love. I had a closer relationship with her than with her son.

"If you stay until after the baby is born, and let my mother have a grand baby, you can stay on my insurance, and I will pay for everything. What do you say?"

I wanted to say *no!* I wanted to go upstairs, pack my things and run to David's arms. Then I felt her flutter in my belly.

"I love your mom," I said softly. "She loves babies so much. She should have a grandchild."

Without discussing it with David or anyone else, I agreed to stay until the baby came. Elden made one more demand: that I should have no contact with David while I remained under his roof. *His roof!* Of course, not mine or ours. I said nothing. It was a devil's bargain, one that proved impossible to keep.

Elden's mother, Lela, delighted in the pending little miracle. She sewed quilts and booties. Earl, Elden's father, built a beautiful wooden cradle and little wooden toys. Elden remained distant, rarely even speaking to me. I continued my studies at the university.

Though I described my devil's bargain to David, it failed after a week. We saw each other in our classes. We met at the botanical gardens, walking among the greenery, holding hands, and talking about the future.

David accompanied me to birthing class on Thursday evenings

since Elden had to work, then we went to *Olde World Cafe* to listen to our friend Sally Rogers sing. We would sit, leaning on one another in a booth, as David wrapped his arms around my swollen belly while we sang along.

When it came time for the birth, Elden accompanied me to the hospital. David could not attend. I longed for him and his loving comfort as tiny Rachael BrieEllen emerged into this world.

That night, alone in my room, I called David and told him that our daughter had come. We both wept.

David, Rachael, and I spent as much time together as possible. We became the family of my dreams, though it was only pretend. David nurtured both Rachael and me, though we always had to return to Howell. I led two completely separate lives. I couldn't wait to leave my old identity as Elden's wife behind forever. I couldn't wait to become a forever family with David and our baby girl.

Elden continued to question my ability to live independently, especially with a baby. He asked if I had thought about where I would live or how I would finish my degree. Having learned from my experience when he tried to sabotage my entrance exams, I kept my inquiries for housing at MSU and all my other plans to myself.

I secured a unit in married housing, arranged with the Women's Legal Aid Clinic to process my divorce, and began packing my things.

Elden begged me to wait until after Christmas, again leveraging my love for his mother.

"Please let her have at least one Christmas before breaking her heart."

Though I did not want to spend another day separated from David, again I agreed.

David, losing hope that I would ever leave Howell, joined Douglas and Patricia in the mountains near Mexico City for two weeks over Christmas. In his absence, I asked my new friends in Lansing to help Rachael and me move into our apartment on campus.

Elden begged me to stay. Lela begged me to stay. With my car fully packed, I apologized, strapped Rachael in her car seat, and drove away forever. I wept as I left for the last time until I entered the freeway. Then, I wiped my eyes and set my sights on my life's next chapter.

The night David returned from Mexico, I invited him to a candle-light dinner in my apartment. We talked about the transition. We thought it best if he continued to live at his own house so I could have space to regroup and establish my independence. We decided on that plan. It sounded like a good plan. However, after that first night, David never left. We joked about how he had come for dinner and stayed forever.

━━•⁘•⋯⁙•➤

I finished school and applied for my teaching certificate. My aunt Pat worked at a Catholic school in Chicago, where she helped me get an interview. I was hired to teach at Saint Eugene's in Chicago. I finished my last exam in the summer session on Thursday, then moved back into my parent's house to begin teaching on the following Tuesday.

My sister Colleen watched Rachael while I worked until David joined us, and we found an apartment closer to my school.

Life together proved sweet and fruitful. I loved having my family so close. Unlike Elden, David loved my family, especially my mother. Though we had little money, we had good friends, good music, family, and each other. We wanted another baby, so we decided to get married.

I loved David. I loved our family. I loved my job. I loved our life. I had never felt truly happy before. After two years, we welcomed Zachary Morgan, then, two years after that, Arra Onelia. Our life included every-thing we needed, but my body continued to betray me. Navigating the city grew more and more challenging for me physically. I didn't know how to rectify that.

We lived on the second floor of a brick two-flat. Climbing the flights of stairs grew more arduous for me, especially as our family grew. One weekend musician friends came to town for a gig and stayed at our flat.

After making the arduous climb to our apartment, having to set my bag of groceries on the stairs above me, then drag myself up, and repeat until I reached the door exhausted, I felt discouraged.

"I've gotta get out of Dodge," I said offhandedly, closing the door behind me.

Our friend Frank, one of the guys in the band who lived in northern lower Michigan, latched on to my words.

"Would you seriously consider moving out of Chicago?" he inquired.

"In a New York minute!" I replied.

CHAPTER 18: ECHOS

['e-()kōs] *plural transitive verb*, to be reminiscent of.

FRANK TOLD ME ABOUT THE SCHOOL IN CADILLAC, where he taught. He informed me of a big turnover happening in the spring, and told me they needed teachers badly. He added that he would love to work with me. After living and teaching in Chicago for several years with three small children, we decided to take the leap.

Sister Carol, the newly-hired principal who lived outside of Milwaukee at the time, met me at a diner off I-94 for my interview. We had a long conversation over coffee. She offered me the job on the spot. The following week I gave my notice at Saint Eugene's, and we began to pack for our move to a brand new place.

David's folks had lived in a nearby town where his father pastored at the United Methodist Church, so he knew the area somewhat, but I had no experience there other than a short visit for Frank and Shelley's wedding a couple of years prior. I felt excited for the adventure and opportunity.

We stored our belongings in Frank and Shelley's barn, and we camped out in their yard, in our tiny, bare-bones, 1960s pop-up with a canvas top throughout the summer while we searched for a place to live. At last, we found our home on Crippen Street in Cadillac, and I began preparing for a new teaching experience at the local Catholic school.

I loved it there. It had one class of each grade, K-5. Sister Carol had an open mind and a love of children and learning. Her pedagogy made an excellent environment for a creative teacher such as myself. I learned the first-grade curriculum, set up my classroom at the end of the building, and readied myself for a new adventure.

Before classes began, I attributed the uneasy feeling in my gut to nervousness about a new place and job. Still, as time passed, I began to realize that the uneasy feeling arose each time I entered the school building. It dissipated as I left. Soon I acknowledged that what I felt was not anxiety but spirit.

Needing to get my children home after school, I couldn't stay late to prepare weekly lessons. I went in on Sunday afternoons instead, spending a couple of uninterrupted hours preparing for the week ahead.

Often, alone in the building, I would hear the sound of children laughing and playing. More than once, I left my classroom, certain that someone occupied the gym, or that another teacher had come in to work with her children in tow. Each time, I searched only to find the building empty of any living soul.

One Sunday afternoon, I heard both adult and children's voices coming from the other end of the hall. The staff had an agreement with one another to notify each other of our presence, given the creepy nature of the building, so I got up from my table and went to the door, intending to do just that. The voices stopped abruptly as I reached the doorway. I waited a few minutes, then returned to my desk. The moment I sat down, I heard it again. Standing up, I looked through the window to see if the sound came from children playing outside, but I could only see the narrow sidewalk and the hospital across the street. I could still hear the voices, so I returned to the door. Once again, the instant I reached the hall, it fell silent.

From my classroom doorway I could see the entire hallway and every classroom door. The windows in each door appeared darkened, and the rooms empty. Still, I bravely decided to walk down the hall to the opposite end just to make sure no one else was in the building. After flipping on the hallway lights, I made my way down the long corridor.

My anxiety increased with every step as the air began to feel thicker. I unlocked each door to check inside every classroom, the office, and the gym. I investigated both the girl's and boy's restrooms. Seeing no one, I called out, "Okay. I know you are here. I'm just doing some work in my classroom, so please stop messing with me!"

Then I turned and walked back down the hall. The moment I reached my classroom, I heard a loud BANG like a door slamming shut. I quickly turned around to see no movement and every door closed. Then, before I could turn to enter my own classroom, I heard it again and again. It sounded as if each door slammed from some distant place, one after the other, coming closer and closer to me.

With my heart in my throat, I raced to my desk, pulled on my coat, and grabbed my things. Fortunately, the exit was right next to my classroom. I surrendered to the spirits and headed out the door as quickly as possible.

As a new teacher, I didn't know my colleagues very well yet, so I felt uneasy asking them if they too experienced odd or frightening things in the building. After getting to know Kevin, the custodian, better, I asked him if he felt anything strange at night when he worked alone. Grateful to have someone who would listen and believe him, he enthusiastically told me of several encounters he had experienced. He said that one night, while working late after BINGO in the gym, he heard voices whispering just outside the restroom door.

"Who's there?" He called, quickly checking the long hallway.

Seeing no one, he returned to his mopping. Then he heard a door slam, and footsteps running in the darkened gym. He also heard more voices, children's voices.

Thinking that someone had broken in, he wasted no time and called the police. Officers arrived in minutes. He accompanied them as they did a thorough sweep of the entire building, including the storage area under the stage, every classroom, closet, office, and restroom. They also checked the crawl space beneath the building but found not a living soul.

"I know what I heard." Kevin insisted.

"Well," the officer assured him, "Maybe they left when they realized you were here. You're working later than usual tonight, right? Give us a call if you hear or see anything else."

After the police left, Kevin quickly finished up and hurried home, locking the building securely behind himself.

This same thing happened multiple times until he finally stopped reporting it to the police and began calling us instead. On more than one occasion Kevin would beg David to help him finish up when something frightened him in the night.

My own experiences continued as did those of others. My daughter, Arra, was in my first-grade class at Saint Ann's. Arra had a keen sensitivity to things both seen and unseen. She openly spoke about feeling uneasy and anxious in parts of the school and classroom. I always assured her that she needn't worry and that nothing would harm her.

Arra also had an uncanny ability to communicate with animals. She understood them on a telepathic level, and they, her. One winter day, Arra brought her bird, Tiny, in for show-and-tell. Tiny had intermittent bouts of anxiety in the classroom which concerned Arra. She did not want to leave him alone in the empty classroom during lunch and recess so I allowed her to remain indoors. She asked if her friends, Kayla and Molly, could stay with her. I agreed, and left them to take my much-needed break.

While the girls sat coloring at the small group table near my desk, they began to hear unusual sounds. Tiny began to flutter about anxiously and squawk from his perch. Arra asked Tiny what was wrong as all the girls began to grow frightened.

Thinking that the sounds came from the school public address system, they looked to the speaker mounted near the crucifix above a bank of wooden closet doors. Suddenly, the crucifix swung from side to side as the closet doors rattled from within.

The three girls grew terrified and grabbed each other's hands. Tiny continued to raise a terrible racket. The terrified little girls jumped to their feet, holding hands for safety. All at once an apparition emerged from the closed, wooden closet doors. It manifested as a woman dressed in white, with a white veil. She clasped her hands in front of herself with her head tilted down toward the floor and began to glide slowly toward the terrified girls.

All three broke ranks and ran screaming toward the door with Kayla in the rear.

The second-grade teacher, hearing the commotion, emerged from her classroom in time to find Arra and Molly screaming and shaking. Suddenly, from just inside the first grade classroom, they heard Kayla scream in pain.

Hearing the kerfuffle, my colleagues and I rushed from the library which served as our break room, to see what caused it. Seeing my girls with the second-grade teacher, I hurried toward them, followed by the principal.

When we reached them, Kayla sobbed uncontrollably, holding her upper arm.

"What on Earth?" I implored."

The girls ran to me, clinging tightly.

"A bride came out of the wall and grabbed Kayla!" Arra cried.

"A bride? What kind of bride?" I asked.

"A BRIDE! A mean bride dressed all in white. She was really mad! She just floated out of the closet. We all ran away, but she grabbed Kayla's arm!"

By this time, the principal had joined us. My fellow teachers appeared frightened, wide-eyed, and tight-mouthed.

"What were you doing when she came out of the wall?" I asked.

Arra replied, "Nothing. We were just coloring. Then Tiny freaked out, and we heard scary noises. Then the cross moved. Then the bride attacked us. This place is haunted!" She insisted.

The second-grade teacher asked Molly if this was true.

"I don't know," she replied, casting her eyes toward the floor.

"But Mom," Arra begged, "It did happen! We all know that this place is haunted. That mean bride came out of the wall. Molly and I ran, but she grabbed Kayla and wouldn't let go!"

Kayla, still sobbing, rubbed her upper arm.

"Did she hurt you?" I asked.

Kayla nodded her head and pushed up her sleeve. An evident imprint of an adult hand wrapped around Kayla's upper arm.

"Okay, okay, that's enough." Sister Ann, our new principal, interjected. "Let's go back into your classroom and take care of this."

The other teachers watched as Sister Ann, three frightened little girls, and I disappeared into my classroom, then they returned nervously to finish their lunches.

"So," asked Sister Ann, "describe what this bride looked like."

Arra explained that she wore a long white dress and a squarish white "head thing" with a veil. She said that they saw blue surrounding her veil and body.

Sister Ann went pale, and shot me a worried glance.

To my astonishment, Sister Ann said, "Okay, let's say some prayers together to make it go away."

The four of us stood in my classroom on a bright winter day as Sister Ann led us in several prayers of protection and simple exorcism. Gradually the little girls calmed down.

"Now," she stated, "Let's not say any more about this! Do you hear me?"

"Yes, Sister." All three little girls replied in unison.

I felt certain I was about to receive a tongue lashing for leaving the children unattended as Sister Ann, looking quite concerned, called me into the hall while the rest of my class returned from recess.

"Did you hear the description of the ghost?" She whispered. "Those girls described exactly the old traditional habit of a Dominican nun! That's my order! That's the order that started this school. They taught here forever! How would the children have known that? How could they make that up—even if they were just scaring themselves?"

Relieved and speechless, I shook my head and shrugged as she went on.

"You know, I've felt scared here sometimes when I stay to work late in my office. It feels like somebody's watching me." She shuddered, "Those old nuns really could be mean! Trust me; I've had that painful arm squeeze before." She laughed nervously. "If we hear from the other moms, I'll tell them that the kids scared themselves."

Then, as she turned to leave, she said half under her breath, "I sure hope those prayers work."

After that infamous incident, the staff began to openly share their unexplained experiences in the school. All, it seemed, had frightening stories to tell.

After the parish built a new church across town, plans ensued to construct a state-of-the-art school building adjacent. Perhaps it was the fact that we all acknowledged the presence of something unseen, or maybe the constant talk about moving that caused a marked increase in spirit activity, but whatever the reason, weird incidents began to ramp up.

One Sunday afternoon in January, I went into school to work on end-of-semester report cards. David needed our only car, so he dropped me off with instructions to call when I needed a ride home. Though I never felt comfortable in the building alone, my task required time to work without interruption from my young family.

Even with the bright sun shining through the windows, my class-room felt chilly. Thermostats in the building were set low on weekends to save energy costs. Following a tip from another teacher who often worked on weekends, I tried to override the room setting by covering the thermostat with a damp paper towel. This, I hoped, would trigger the heat to come on. After nearly thirty minutes, the abrupt sound of the register kicking on startled me so much, I jumped in my seat.

With my heart still racing, I rubbed my icy hands together to warm the stiffness, and pulled my scarf tighter around my neck. Though heat poured from the register under the bank of windows, the chair, table top, walls, and my body still felt frozen.

Shuddering, I returned to my work. I wanted to finish as quickly and efficiently as possible so I could return home to spend the rest of Sunday afternoon and evening with my family.

Nearing the end of my stack of report cards, I began to hear an unfamiliar sound. I cocked my head, and focused my attention toward it. At first, I thought it came from the blower, but when the fan in the registers stopped, the other sound continued. I stood up to look outside, hoping to find something there to explain it. It sounded like static as if a radio was tuned between stations. The heat had barely put a dent in the chill. I stood, shivering, and listening closely, trying to determine its source.

Then a distant, crackly voice became audible under the static. I suddenly realized that it came from the PA speaker on the wall above the crucifix. The ancient school PA system, a throwback from the early 1960s, was located in the principal's office. To operate it, one had to switch it on, wait several minutes for the tubes to warm up, then push a button to speak into a vintage microphone mounted on a short table stand. It was not the kind of thing that could accidentally turn on by itself. Listening more closely, I began to make out a woman's voice. Though I could not decipher any words, it sounded more and more distressed.

Perhaps the radio station is bleeding through, I thought, but the voice grew more urgent.

"That's no radio station," I declared to the empty room.

The hair on my arms and the back of my neck stood on end as I stared at the dusty beige speaker and tried to decipher the words garbled amidst the static that seemed to grow louder and louder every minute. Then I thought I heard the words, "Help me."

Maybe there's an emergency in the office. Perhaps somebody needs my help. I thought.

Wondering if perhaps Sister Ann or somebody else had fallen and tried to use the PA system to get help, I quickly made my way to the office to investigate. I heard nothing in the hallway or coming from any of the other rooms as I pulled out my master key to open the office door.

The outer office was dark and still. Goosebumps rose on my skin, and my heart raced as I fumbled with the key unlocking Sister Ann's inner office. Nothing. No one. Not a living soul. The PA system was switched off. I touched it to see if it felt warm, since the old apparatus heated up considerably when in use. Cold. Everything around me remained silent and cold. A rush of adrenaline surged through my body as fear pierced my consciousness.

Who the Hell? I thought, *What the Hell!?*

Pulling the doors behind me, I headed back to my classroom, determined not to let whatever bled through the speaker deter me from completing my task. I tried to convince myself that it must be picking up random radio signals, though I had never experienced that from the speaker before. When I got back to my room, I found that the static and disembodied voice had ceased. Relieved, I closed my classroom door to retain the small amount of heat generated by the heater which had been blowing. My classroom felt more frigid than ever despite my attempt to thwart the system.

I had three, maybe four reports to go, so I pushed myself to wind up my work for the day. Shock overtook me as the speaker abruptly blasted static at an ear-shattering decibel! I leapt to my feet, terrified. Then the voice, clearer now, began,

"He-e-e-lp." It pleaded, followed by illegible uttering, then "O-o-o-ut! Help—out."

That settled it. I was *done*. OUT! Shaking, I dialed home only to get the answering machine.

Shit! I thought, looking at the clock. *They won't be back for a while.*

Still I had no intention of remaining in that building. I left a message on the answering machine telling David to please pick me up as soon as possible. Then, leaving the unfinished report cards on the table, I bundled up and hightailed it out of the building to wait on the porch in the frozen January sunshine.

CHAPTER 19: REPRIEVE

[ri-ˈprēv] *noun*, a temporary respite (as from pain or trouble)

EVERYTHING CHANGED IN MY THIRTY-EIGHTH YEAR. I had struggled with physical disability and a bleak prognosis since adolescence. Then I watched a science program on public television. It showed a woman from Lyme, Connecticut, who suffered from a mysterious crippling disease. Her story matched mine in so many ways. In the end, scientists discovered that a spirochete bacteria injected from a tick bite had caused her malady. A course of antibiotics cured her.

Tick bite! I spent every summer of my childhood in the north woods of Wisconsin, suffering many tick bites. I wondered, hoped even, could this be the case for me?

Not ten minutes after the conclusion of the program, the phone rang.

"Tiyi, it's Mom. I was just watching this program on PBS about a woman with severe arthritis caused by a tick bite."

"I know!" I exclaimed, "I saw it too! Do you think that might be what I have?"

"It could be." She replied. "God knows you've had enough ticks. Right?"

"Right," I laughed.

"You should look into it. Maybe, just maybe, there's a cure for you."

"I will." I promised, "I'll do some research and talk to my doctor."

"Keep me posted." She said.

"Of course," I replied, and hung up the phone.

The next day after school, I went to the public library to begin a deep dive through the microfiche in search of articles in medical journals related to this newly-discovered malady named Lyme Disease, after the place where it was first discovered. Whenever I came across something promising, I tagged and printed it. After several hours I had, in my possession, a stack of research articles and case studies. Placing them carefully in my briefcase, I returned home.

The next morning, I made an appointment with my doctor.

Doctor Bill Grace's son was one of my first graders. We had a warm and friendly relationship.

"Hi, Teach!" He said cheerily, "What can I do for you today?"

"What do you know about Lyme Disease?" I asked.

"Not much." He replied, "I've heard of it, but I really don't know anything about it. Why?"

Pulling the stack of copies from my briefcase, I said, "Here. Read these and let me know what you think."

"Ah, homework from the teacher. Okay," he laughed, fanning the pages. "I will."

"Great, " I replied, "That's all I've got for now."

"Did you read these articles?" He asked.

"Of course."

"What do *you* think?"

"Read them. This sounds promising."

He agreed, and I left, feeling excited and hopeful for the first time in forever.

The next day I received a call from Doctor Grace's nurse. She told me that his last patient would be done at seven and asked me to come in after that for a consultation.

He seemed excited when he came into the room.

"We could have something here," He said, smiling. "I'm not sure how to go about testing. There are blood tests, but they are often inaccurate. Let me talk to one of my friends who works on infectious diseases, figure out a protocol, and get back to you with what we need to do next."

"I really think this is it." I said, "The case study in *The New England Journal* is my story exactly. Just put it in Wisconsin, change the name, and everything reported happened to me."

"I know," he said gently, "but this is all so new. I don't want you to get your hopes up if it doesn't pan out. Still let's follow this through okay?"

"Okay," I said, ignoring his advice about my hopes.

A whirlwind followed, including advice from one of Dr. Grace's medical school colleagues in the east, blood tests, and more research. I imagined what my life without crippling pain and disability would look like. I began making lists of things I could not do that I wished I could, throwing Grammie Ethel's, as well as my doctor's advice to the wind. I imagined myself riding a bike, attending museums and zoos on foot instead of in a wheelchair, and taking walks alone in the woods. I envisioned carrying my baby while holding the hand of his sister, instead of needing one hand for my cane. I imagined energy, clarity, and the normal life of a young woman, something I had never experienced. For the first time since I sat in the chair across from the doctor who gave me a death sentence at age fifteen, I imagined growing old.

It took two weeks for the bloodwork results to arrive. I got a call from the doctor's office to come in and made an appointment for the following day with my heart full of hope.

The results, however, came back negative. My heart dropped and I felt tears well up as I sat in the exam room looking down at the floor.

That night, Friday, I arrived home feeling hopeless and depressed. Telling David the terrible news, I got into bed and refused to get up the next day. Then Mom called me.

"What's going on?" She asked, "I can tell something is wrong."

In tears, I told her about the Lyme test results.

Mom remained silent for a few minutes, then said, "I'm so sorry, Tiyi. That really stinks."

I told her how I had begun making lists of things I couldn't do for the first time. I told her I felt foolish to even hope for anything else. I told her that I didn't want to get out of bed. Ever."

"Aw, my Tiyi," she soothed, "I know this is just terrible. You have every right to feel sorry for yourself and wallow in self-pity, but only do that for twenty-four hours. After that, you need to remember that nothing is different from the day before your test results. Remember that you have a wonderful family that loves you and that you are a remarkable woman who can do anything. That can't change with a blood test result, right?"

After hanging up, I pulled the covers back up over my head, then began thinking,

Before I had ever even heard of Lyme disease, I loved my life. I loved teaching, my husband, kids, friends, music, and community. I still had everything that made me happy and fulfilled. The only thing that had changed was that I had more information.

I pulled off the covers, washed my face, got dressed, and resolved to keep on with whatever lay before me. I still had a lot to learn and do in whatever time I had in this life. *Every living moment ...* I reminded myself

✦✳⋯⋰⋯✦

On Monday, I received a call from Doctor Grace to come in that evening.

"So," He said, "I learned that these Lyme Titer tests have a track record of 60% false negatives. Your other tests indicate the presence of an infection, an unspecified infection. It could still be the *Borrelia spiro-chete*. This is not conclusive."

Though his words rang with possibilities, I tried to keep my hopes in check.

"My friend told me about a clinical test we can do. Are you game?" He asked.

"What's that?"

"Well, rheumatoid arthritis does not respond to antibiotics," he said, "So, let's do a round of the recommended medicine and see what happens."

I agreed, promising to keep a daily journal of how I felt while on the antibiotics, and report back in three to four weeks.

Driving home, I prayed for this to work. I prayed for relief. I prayed for possibilities. The next day I began taking large doses of doxycycline. Every day I wrote how I felt in the morning and at night. I wrote about my pain levels, heat in my joints, and swelling. In the beginning, I felt sick to my stomach and extremely foggy and weak. I called the doctor's office to see if maybe I had an allergy to the antibiotic. I had rarely taken antibiotics previously in my life, and had some other medications that did cause a reaction. Without a rash, the nurse instructed me to keep going.

After nearly three weeks, I needed to make some copies for my classroom one afternoon. I had only a few minutes before the kids would return from lunch so I took what I needed to copy and began making my way down the hallway toward the office, forgetting to grab my cane.

"Wow!" Frank exclaimed, smiling, "You're moving at quite a clip!"

Suddenly realizing that, not only had I left my cane behind, but I walked swiftly and without pain, I declared gleefully, "I sure am! Woohoo!"

As soon as I reached the office, I called my doctor to give him the news.

"I have no pain!" I reported. "I can move really well!"

I told him what Frank had observed.

"Great," he said, "Stop taking the doxy and keep close tabs on how you are feeling."

After four days without the medicine, I woke up and could barely move. My knees appeared hot and severely swollen. My hands throbbed with pain. I felt as if I had collided with a truck.

Oh NO! I thought. *It's back. The antibiotics didn't work.*

I left a message with Doctor Grace, and spent the rest of the day getting reacquainted with the cruel pain I had endured for decades.

That evening I returned to the doctor's office and waited in the exam room.

To my surprise, he entered gleefully.

"BINGO!" He exclaimed.

"What?" I asked puzzled, "It didn't work. As soon as I stopped taking the medicine it came back with a vengeance!"

"That's great!" He said, "That was supposed to happen if it was the *Borrelia spirochete*. This is just so exciting!"

Next, we had to navigate insurance companies. The recommended treatment included intravenous drug infusions that would cost over ten thousand dollars. Lyme disease was new and controversial, and the treatment experimental at best, plus a negative blood test might give the insurance company more than enough ammunition to refuse to cover the treatment.

Finally, the drugs were approved with a proven diagnosis of severe systemic infection, though only in a hospital inpatient setting.

I needed to work and support my family, my baby Ezra. I could not languish in a hospital bed for weeks to receive the infusions.

After more calls and convincing, the insurance company agreed to pay for the drugs, but not the home health care needed to monitor a piggyback IV pump. Fortunately for me my community rallied and a couple of home health nurses with children in or formerly in my class volunteered to stop in every day to make sure things continued to go well. I began treatment.

After a few weeks of daily infusions, I became violently ill cycling between terrible chills and unbearable heat, interspersed with periods of unconsciousness. My doctor ordered me to stop treatment. I went to bed and slept for more than twenty-four hours.

When I finally awoke, I felt disoriented and weak. I lay perfectly still, startled by the fact that I could not feel my body. Fearing paralysis, I hesitated to move. At last I moved my hand, then my neck, then feet and legs. I realized that what I felt was not lack of feeling, but lack of pain.

For the first time that I could remember I felt no pain. Swelling in my hands and knees had all but vanished. I sat on the edge of the bed, feeling slightly dizzy from my ordeal, and called to David.

He rushed into the room, clearly concerned, and asked what I needed.

"It worked," I said as my eyes welled up, "It's gone. I don't hurt."

Chapter 20: Remembrance

[ri-'mem-brən(t)s] *noun*, an act of recalling to mind.

MY FORTIETH YEAR BEGAN WITH RENEWED STRENGTH AND HOPE. After suffering for most of my life with a terminal misdiagnosis, and painful disabling symptoms, at last, I faced the possibility of living a full life. Though irreparable damage had occurred in my body, I entered my forties with more strength and energy than I had known since childhood.

With this new energy also came a time of psychic and spiritual reawakening. A series of remarkable dreams began haunting my sleep, gradually revealing memories of a part of me that I had long forgotten.

The first series of dreams began with music. Deafening, resonant, dissonant music that hurt my ears and fiercely invaded my senses. In the midst of this overwhelming cacophony, I found myself standing naked before a sea of multiple and endless vivid colors. Though the colors swirled and undulated wildly, each color remained intact without blending with or muting the colors surrounding it. Each color appeared as small, brightly colored, individual moving organisms.

I stood, reluctant to enter this mass of overstimulation, but gingerly stepped forward into it. The moment my feet submerged into the colors, I felt an electric buzzing. The liquid burned, froze, tingled, pierced, and tickled—all at once. I tried to take another step, but I could not tolerate the excruciating intensity, feeling like I might lose my mind. As I backed away from it, I awoke instantly.

Lying motionless in my bed, I attempted to decipher the meaning of what I had just experienced in my dream. I felt drained of energy and could not muster an explanation. Glancing at the clock on my bedside table, I watched it change to 3:00 AM. Turning over, I relaxed and drifted back to sleep.

Several nights later I again found myself standing before that sea of cacophony and color. Once more, the overwhelming sound drowned out all thought. Again I stepped into the swirling mass of intense stimuli. Knowing what to expect made the first steps both terrifying and surprisingly easier to take. I took one step, holding my hands and arms high to avoid contact with the swirling and shifting sea of color, Then another, and another until the vibrating, viscous substance reached my thighs. I tried to continue knowing that I must, but I could tolerate no more. Once again, I awoke suddenly, lying on my back in my warm, soft bed.

David snored quietly beside me. I felt troubled by the recurrence of this disturbing dream, knowing that it held significant meaning for me though it remained a mystery. Again, the illuminated clock on the bedside table read 3:00. This, too, had significance, I thought. I lay awake for nearly an hour before falling into a dreamless sleep, waking hours later to my alarm. This ordeal repeated several nights each week, with me stepping further and deeper into the colors by minute increments, always awakening at, or near 3:00 AM.

Then, after several weeks free of my troubling dream, I found myself on that strange beach once more. As the music assaulted my ears and mind, I found that if I hummed a sustained harmonic pitch, discordant noise ceased to cause me pain. Adding my own voice to the cacophony made it bearable. I had an epiphany that becoming part of it instead of trying to avoid the sensation made it a completely different experience. I looked at the colors before me, moving so that one could interpret it to both beckon, and repel all at the same time. For the first time, I noticed pebbles covering the beach. I could feel each one individually vibrating through the soles of my bare feet. They felt warm and surprisingly comfortable, even pleasant.

Still humming, I lifted my arms and began my journey into the mysterious sea. The stimulation felt less painful. I focused on joining with, and adding to the unusual colors engulfing my body. I ventured past my waist. My heart raced, and my breath quickened. Looking at my hands, I cupped them and dipped them deeply into the swirling mass of colors. Then I lifted my full hands upward and watched the vibrant colors run down my arms and onto my body. Though the sensation had not diminished, I found it not at all painful but exciting, almost orgasmic. I smiled and began turning around and around in the midst of the wildness. I could no longer see the shore but found myself completely engulfed by wild colors and cacophonous discordant music. Lifting my face toward the sky, I realized that it consisted of billowing, rotating clouds, also of vibrant color. I reached down again, lifting handfuls of the liquid colors, and poured them onto my head and body. Next, I leaned back and slipped entirely into the sea. As my face submerged, The music disappeared, and I became one with the swirling colors.

All at once, I remembered a pivotal event from my early childhood when I heard fairies calling my name. I followed and let my spirit dance with the beautiful cloud-like beings. I glided over, then slipped into and became the lake itself, experiencing its vastness and wonder-filled essence. My dream felt like that time and that lake, only ... not in this world. I had stepped into a place similar but far more vivid than in my temporal existence. The churning "sea" of colors was my soul, my spirit swirling with all the possibilities of the universe. I felt I was immersed into a baptism of the mysteries of the hidden world. I felt my body rising toward, then beyond the surface. My eyes remained closed as the disso-nant music suddenly made perfect sense, and I recognized it as the fairy music I had heard long ago. It filled the vastness of space of which I now had become part. I had traversed through the gate and into a whole new reality.

Smiling blissfully, I opened my eyes. The color synthesized into golden light, then faded to darkness. I noticed, but remained unfazed by the appearance of two moons mirroring each other. I floated effort-lessly in the blackness of space, in this new reality between two moons, knowing that I had found a pathway into it. I felt triumphant, and peaceful, floating timelessly.

When I awoke, I heard birdsong. Bright morning sun sparkled on dew in the crabapple tree outside my bedroom window. I lay for a long time, recalling every detail of my dream. I understood its meaning. I understood that trickles of secrets, like the tiny bits of swirling color, had revealed themselves to me throughout my lifetime. I smiled, anticipating wonderful and mysterious things ahead.

CHAPTER 21: RECRUDESCENCE

[ˌrē-krü-ˈde-sᵊn(t)s] *noun*, breaking out afresh or into renewed activity,
revival or reappearance in active existence.

WITH A NEW UNDERSTANDING OF WONDERS that lay just beyond the physically visible, I began to recall memories of my ancestors, or of lives I had experienced thousands of years ago. I started practicing rituals from my memories or from my ancestors, or perhaps my spirit guides who have accompanied me on this journey through many lifetimes.

Sacred objects fell into my path, and I gratefully placed them on my growing altar space. I began opening myself up to lessons long forgotten. I remembered words and places, people, mystery, and myself.

Summertime found me staying in a small cottage across the lake from where I had first encountered the fairies. David and I had volunteered to supervise the older campers at Granny's Camp Up North, where all my mother's grandchildren spent two weeks together. The group of children had grown to twenty between the ages of one and twelve. To allow more freedom for the older campers, and more space for the littles, we took the older children to Camp Jackpine. The big kids slept in a bunkhouse, and David and I occupied a cottage adjacent.

One weekend David had to return to Michigan for work while I remained to tend the children. Alone in the cottage, I awoke suddenly just before dawn. The foot of the queen size bed faced a large picture window looking over a steep hillside that dropped to the shore of the lake. Putting on my glasses as I sat up in the warm bed, I noticed the lake completely obscured by a mist that undulated in the gentle pre-dawn breeze.

"The fairy mist!" I exclaimed aloud.

I quickly jumped out of bed, pulled off my nightgown, and wrapped up in my robe. Stepping into flip flops by the screen door, I silently made my way down the path past the bunkhouse where the children remained sleeping in the predawn hour. The air felt thick with a morning chill and the sweet scent of Jackpine as I followed the stone steps and sandy, pine needle-covered path through the mist to the lakeshore. I walked along the beach until the cottages on the hillside stood well behind me.

My nerves tingled as I stepped out of my flip-flops, placing my bare feet on the cool, moist sand. I felt adrenaline pulse through my veins, and a flutter filled my belly as I faced the water. Removing my glasses rendered the world all-around into a mystical pastel. I did not need to see with my eyes. I wanted to see with my third eye. I wanted to make my way again through the awaiting gate.

Closing my eyes, I heard faint stirrings of a far-off symphony, music I recognized. Music I remembered. I began to hum the harmonic, then opened my eyes to see the same beings I had encountered as a little girl. I was no longer a child. I greeted them as the woman I had become, the woman I had been. Dropping my robe in the sand, and naked, I entered the cool still water slowly, precariously, determined to not disturb the glass-like surface. Suddenly, I felt gripped by a powerful memory. The memory of performing this ancient ritual thousands of times—thousands of years in the distant past—flooded my psyche. Tears began streaming down my face as I lifted it toward the heavens and the beings that welcomed me back.

Dipping my hands into the water, I recalled the sacred words of blessing, and lifted my cupped hands high above my head, letting the cool water cascade down my arms. I felt euphoric and one with all things. The water, catching the early morning light, appeared as liquid gold running down my body. I stood, palms upward, accepting the blessing of the earth, sky, and water. Remembering the ritual, I turned my hands over. My palms faced down and my fingertips aimed toward the vastness of the universe just as the tip of the sun reached the treetops across the lake. I felt a charge of power as golden light radiated from my fingertips into the sky, returning brilliant streaks of light to the awakening sun.

The ritual ended abruptly at the terrifying sound of a large, golden retriever jumping, barking, and growling threateningly from the shore. I spun around quickly, now shivering, completely exposed, and naked in the shallow water. The ferocity of the creature startled me. Golden retrievers rarely attack non-threatening strangers. This one wore a red bandanna around its neck, which should have made it seem more ridiculous than threatening, but it leapt and growled, ready to attack. I assumed it had witnessed my ritual, and that perhaps the power of joining my light with the light of the rising sun had frightened it. Fearing an attack, I backed slowly away, deeper into the water.

Suddenly I heard crashing through the brush on the steep hillside along the shore that drew my attention away from the threat directly in front of me. All at once Dana Dog leapt from a height of about seven feet, landing directly in front of the threatening dog. Dana Dog bared her teeth, and growled viciously, lunging at the intruder who, yipping, ran off down the beach.

Dana stood watching my would-be attacker retreat until it disappeared in the waning mist, then she turned toward me and sat at attention next to my waiting robe.

Dana was a remarkable creature. Her human, my friend Bob, who tended the grounds and buildings at camp, called her "Dingo Dog." She appeared wild and wolf-like with mottled gray fur and long legs. She had one blue and one brown eye that seemed to pierce my soul as I stood waist-deep in the chilly morning lake.

"Good girl, Dana," I said, "Good girl."

Then I made my way, shivering, to the shore. She did not move a muscle as I rubbed her head and thanked her for rescuing me. Pulling my robe around my wet body, I slipped my sandy feet into my flip flops, and made my way back up the path to my cottage. Dana remained close at my side until I reached the screened porch. She sat down outside the screen door as I went in to have a warm shower and get dressed for the day. She remained there until I re-emerged.

Dana stayed at my side for the rest of my time at camp. She came along when I went for walks down the road and she followed me to the kitchen door when I went to the mess hall to prepare breakfast. Dana refused to leave my side. She even slept on the stoop outside my cottage door.

"Looks like Dana chose you over me," Bob remarked jokingly, "You trying to steal my dog?"

"Not me," I replied. "She just seems to want to hang out with me."

Unsure of how he might interpret it, I never told Bob about the early morning incident when Dana The "Dingo Dog" defended me from imminent peril. Just as I believed the retriever had seen my ritual and became terrified, I also believed that Dana had witnessed that power and, as I had, remembered.

Dana watched as we drove away after that summer of awakening. Though long ago and far away, I dream of her often, feeling a deep connection to her wild protective nature, and the mystery we shared. From that day forward, she became my most powerful spirit animal, my guardian, and companion into the spirit realm, always ready to protect and defend me against peril as I learn, grow, and continue to emerge as a gatekeeper.

CHAPTER 22: INVEIGLE

[in-'vā-gəl] *transitive verb*, to entice, lure, or ensnare by inducements.

THE NEXT SUMMER, MY UNCLE JIM INVITED ALL THE FAMILIES in my generation to spend six weeks at Camp Jackpine. Each family had its own cottage. We shared some meals and events at a common area or lodge and the beach, but each had our private space. Several of my cousins and sisters took advantage of this offer to spend most of the summer Up North together on a beautiful lake. Since most of the dads had to remain behind to work, my sisters, cousins, and I referred to it as Amazon Camp.

David could not stay the entire six weeks because he had a summer gig running sound for the city at the performing arts pavilion back home on several weekends. We became even closer friends with "Builder" Bob during our stay. Dana Dog again followed me throughout the day, though she slept in Bob's cottage with him. Still, I always felt her eyes on me and felt her protection wherever I went.

I continued to feel the freedom of movement and energy afforded me by successfully treating my Lyme disease. As at Granny's Camp, our cottage stood adjacent to the bunkhouse, and we supervised the older children who stayed there.

Trying to concoct a way for David and I to both participate fully in the six week vacation the next summer, and still earn much needed wages, we began to look for places we might play musical gigs during the season. We would only need a few events to replace David's income in the city. Since we shared a love for the kind of music we played, we asked

Bob if he knew of any venues that hosted live acoustic music. Bob said he had made friends with some local musicians who had a gig in Bayfield the following weekend. He suggested we go with him to meet them and see if they had any ideas. Unfortunately, David had to return to Cadillac that weekend, so Bob and I made plans to go together.

We set out for the ninety-minute drive in the late evening to listen to the band. Uncle Jim had stocked the camp garage with fast cars. We chose to take the car we called "The Batmobile," a sleek, black Mazda RX-7.

We enjoyed the music and company at the bar, then stayed to talk to the musicians at the end of the night. It was nearly two o'clock in the morning when we finally said goodbye and pulled away from the bar and the town.

A thick cloud cover obscured any moonbeams or starlight, making it seem that the blackness of the wee hours enveloped us as we headed home on desolate country roads through the expansive pine forest in far northwestern Wisconsin. We sang along with Bob's new CD by one of our mutually favorite artists, Greg Brown, as we made our way through the darkness.

For the better part of an hour, we passed no little towns, cabins, or farmhouses whose lights might break up the blackness of this night. That left only our headlights to cut through a short distance of the abyss directly in front of us, only to swallow up behind us as we made our way home.

I looked at the clock on the dashboard, noticing the late hour.

"I hope we don't pay too dearly tomorrow morning for staying out so late tonight," I said to Bob.

"No sleeping in for us." He chuckled, "I've got work to do, and you will have all those kids bright and early. Either way, that band sure sounded great, didn't it?"

"Sure did." I replied, "but I probably should have used the bathroom before leaving. My bladder situation is hitting critical. How much longer do you think?"

"At least forty minutes, maybe more." He said, "If you like, we can just pull over. We haven't seen another car for at least thirty miles."

"No," I told him, "You can pee in the woods because you have outdoor plumbing, if you know what I mean, but I need someplace to sit."

I lifted the end of my cane to accentuate how squatting in the woods could not happen with my disabilities.

"Just drive quickly," I implored. Maybe we will pass something when we hit the main highway."

Though I spoke the words, I doubted the possibility of finding a place open. In this part of the northern wilderness, few if any establishments remained open after eleven, let alone almost three o'clock in the morning. I took a deep breath, reminding Bob to watch out for deer, but to drive quickly.

My discomfort grew as we reached the main highway. Turning south on the desolate pavement, I comforted myself, knowing that home, and a bathroom, lay just over a half-hour ahead. I could hold on until then. At least I hoped I could.

"Hey, look!" Bob exclaimed, "Does that look open?"

I turned to the direction he indicated. To my great relief, I saw a bright red neon sign for The Roadhouse Saloon not a thousand feet ahead on the left. As we got closer, I noticed the neon beer signs illuminating the windows.

"Yes!" I replied, "And not a moment too soon!"

As we turned off the main highway onto the side road leading to the gravel parking lot, Bob told me that he had heard of this place.

"Everybody is talking about their new mural. I've wanted to get up here but haven't had a chance."

He went on to tell me that folks said some mysterious artist who worked at Disney Studios had painted it, and they all said it was pretty cool. I cared far less about a mural and considerably more about the location of the ladies' room.

As we approached the heavy wooden door, neon signs bathed

the parking lot in red light. I noticed four or five aging cars and trucks parked in the gravel lot.

"Okay you order a couple of beers, I'm heading directly to the ladies' room." I said leaning on my cane to quicken my pace toward the door.

Bob pulled the door open, and we stepped into the warm light of The Roadhouse Saloon. The moment we entered, all eyes turned toward us as if expecting our arrival. I noticed three wrung-out and exhausted-looking ladies sitting silently on barstools with sweating cocktails neglected in front of them. Across the bar sat two gentlemen, a middle-aged fellow with horn-rimmed glasses, and the other an elderly man who looked as if all the color had long since washed out of his face. As we stood near the doorway adjusting to the lighting, a disheveled-looking younger fellow holding a bottle of beer in one hand came careening toward us,

"Hey," he slurred, "C'mon in and have a drink."

He reached up for a "high five" smiling to reveal extremely discolored brownish teeth.

It's late, I thought to myself, *Looks like they've been here a really long time.*

Bob and I both slapped him a "high five," then I maneuvered past him on a beeline to the ladies' room. I smiled at the grinning bartender, whose tight jeans and sleeveless t-shirt exaggerated his broad chest and formidable biceps.

"Welcome folks, what'll it be?" I heard him say as Bob approached the bar.

"Two long-neck cold ones" replied Bob as I entered the bathroom.

The door closed behind me, and I fumbled to find the light switch, hoping that I would make it these last few seconds. I did. Feeling so much better, I flushed, then went to the sink to wash my hands. I couldn't help but notice that the sink was completely dry, and that no paper towels cluttered the small trash receptacle. Looking in the mirror as I scrubbed my hands, I wrinkled up my face in an expression of disgust. I thought about those ladies who had spent many hours on those bar stools. Either they had bladders of steel, or they never washed their hands.

"Gross." I thought, then dismissed my judgment, thinking that maybe somebody had already cleaned it since it had to be near closing time.

Leaving the bathroom, I met Bob at the bar. I noticed two gentlemen, one a short scrawny guy, and the other an enormous mountain of a man, standing silently around a pool game seemingly in progress. I also noticed the mural to my right. It covered every inch of a twenty-foot wall with a scene resembling a western movie backdrop. As I made my way toward my beer in Bob's outstretched hand, the brown-toothed fellow dropped a coin in the jukebox. "Let's Twist Again Like We Did Last Summer" began to play. I took note of the amazingly pristine condition of the vintage Wurlitzer filled with vinyl 45s. I hadn't seen one like that since my childhood, and even way back then, they all looked pretty well-used.

As the music played, every living soul, save for the bartender who leaned far over the top of the bar watching and grinning while swaying his tight-jeaned hips, poured him or herself off their barstools to make their way to the fully lit dance floor. Dancing with no one in particular they stepped or shuffled absently to the beat of the old-time rock 'n roll hit. The younger man teetered toward me, grinning through his brownish discolored teeth and cloudy, unfocused eyes.

"Hey ..." he slurred, "Wanna dance?"

I leaned on my cane as he reached for me.

"Sorry, buddy," I said, pointing to my cane, "I can't."

His face fell, then he turned to stumble out onto the dance floor with the others. When the song finished, the patrons returned to their original positions around the bar, and Bob and I walked across the now empty dance floor toward the mural. I began to feel more and more uncomfortable because, as we did, every eye in the place fixed unflinchingly on Bob and me. Nobody spoke, nobody moved, nobody hit a pool ball, and nobody even lifted a glass for a drink. They just watched us without expression. I moved closer to Bob.

We studied the mural in silence. The painting appeared rough and garish, much like a backdrop for a stage play. It depicted an old west saloon scene complete with swinging doors, gamblers, a piano player in gartered sleeves with a female singer, a muscle-bound gunslinger, an overly made-up lady of the night, and a few more. The lighting seemed to emanate from the floor, creating a tense and disturbing feeling much like a Toulouse-Lautrec painting. The characters glared out from the wall with disproportionate bodies twisted in unnatural, almost agonized poses. I shuddered as I noticed the mixing of grays, greens, pinks, and yellows fading toward the edges of the wall.

After a few short minutes, we heard the sound of another coin drop into the jukebox. For a second time, it played "Let's Twist Again Like We Did Last Summer." Somewhat alarmed, I turned my face slowly to watch as every patron again eased onto to the dance floor. The bartender and pool players grinned at the ladies. One had a blonde bouffant hairdo and red lipstick that bled into the wrinkles on her upper lip. Another had short gray hair and a cracked, aging face. The other woman, who appeared younger, though no less worn, swayed her broad hips as the men at the pool table leered hungrily.

I kept feeling even more uncomfortable. Then Bob nudged me.

"Check it out," he said, drawing my attention back to the mural."

"What?" I responded, trying to split my attention between Bob and the portending activities in the room behind us.

"Look!" he said, forcing my full attention, "Look closely at the people in the mural. They are all here ... In the bar."

"Seriously?" I said, laughing nervously in disbelief.

The song ended, and once again, the people in The Roadhouse Saloon returned silently to their places. I glanced from the mural to one after another around the bar.

"Holy shit!" I said, realizing that every single character in the mural sat or stood somewhere in our immediate presence.

I quickly found the bartender's likeness portraying a musclebound gunslinger sporting a tight shirt with six-shooters strapped to his hips and a black hat tilted rakishly over his brow. The blond bouffant lady stood next to the piano player who bore the grinning face of the brown-toothed guy. The skinny guy, the old gray guy at the bar, and the man wearing horn-rimmed glasses sat at a gambling table playing cards while the younger blonde lady leaned suggestively over the table, exposing ample cleavage. The older lady sat alone with a shot glass and bottle on the table in front of her.

As my anxiety began to rise, Bob nudged me jokingly.

"Hey," he said, "Don't worry. The big guy isn't in the mural, so we're safe."

I felt anything but safe as he went on, "These folks are obviously regulars. I bet the artist used them as models for the painting. What a cool thing to do eh? C'mon," he said, taking my arm to return to the bar, "Let's ask 'em."

I laughed nervously, telling myself what he said made perfect sense, and that my imagination had once again jumped to impossible conclusions. Still, every eye in the place watched as we strode with our backs to the mural to the bartender.

Placing our empty bottles on the bar, Bob smiled in a friendly way and asked the bartender if he had posed for the mural. The bartender just grinned without responding. Then Bob asked about the other folks in the mural. The bartender just stared at us. He clearly could hear us, but he never responded. He just grinned at us without a word.

Figuring that the ladies might talk to another female, I asked across the bar if they were in the mural. They just looked blankly at me. They *all* just stared blankly at us. All of them. Knowing they had heard, it felt all of a sudden as if we spoke a language they did not understand.

"Let's have one for the road," Bob said, "so we can get another look at that mural."

Reluctantly I agreed, wishing instead that we could just get out of there. With fresh bottles in hand, we walked across the dance floor to the back wall and the disconcerting mural. As we approached, I grabbed Bob's arm.

"There's the big guy right there!" I whispered, gesturing to a figure in the mural standing at the far end of the bar polishing a glass with a white towel.

"Oh my God!" Bob whispered loudly with feigned panic in his voice. Then the alarm became real.

"Look there!"

He pointed to the center left of the mural. To my horror, I saw two figures just outside the swinging saloon doors. I couldn't quite make them out at first. They appeared as brushstrokes of mixed colors, much like the edges of the painting. I began to see, however, that the figures depicted a man and a woman. Looking more closely and with great intensity, the colors seemed to move, swirl, and begin filling in. I saw that the woman's skirt seemed to be gaining more pinks and whites.

"Is that us?" Bob leaned in close, pretending to try to scare me.

I pushed him playfully, then turned back to the mural. The figures in the door had changed again and had somehow filled in. I saw the two figures better, though without any facial features. I studied the woman. She had curly hair, a long skirt tinted pink, ankle-high boots, and ... Just then, another coin fell and the only song that played the entire night, "Let's Twist Again ..." began anew.

I noticed that this time the brown-toothed man didn't begin to dance. He just watched us. The men at the pool table just watched us. The bartender and the people at the bar just watched us as the song began to fill the room.

Turning to tell Bob that I wanted to leave, I got one last look at that mural. I needed nothing else.

"LOOK!" I exclaimed loudly. "It IS us! There's my cane."

We had studied all the figures in that mural, looking for matches with folks in the bar. I would have noticed two figures that closely resembled Bob and myself in the doorway, but even if I had missed that, I certainly would not have missed a pink skirted, ankle booted woman with curly hair just like mine walking with a cane.

All at once we shouted, "Let's get the Hell outta here!"

We wasted not a second more but sprinted as best we could toward the doorway. As we did, every person in the bar stood up turning to watch silently. Without a word, we quickly dropped our nearly-full bottles on the edge of the bar as we flew past it on our way to the door to the parking lot. The music played loudly as Bob swung open the heavy door. The young man who played the jukebox began to move toward us.

"Hurry!" Bob said urgently. "C'mon. We've gotta get out of here right now."

As the wooden door shut behind me, I froze in place. I dared not take a single step because when it closed, we found ourselves suddenly in pitch blackness. I feared I might stumble and fall, delaying our escape.

"Don't move," Bob instructed, "I'll turn on the car lights so you can see where to go."

I didn't move. I stood in that abysmal darkness, hearing not a sound. We had escaped in the middle of the song, but as soon as the door slammed shut, everything stopped, and we stood alone in total darkness and silence. Terrified, I hoped that we had actually found our way back to the parking lot and not into some other place or void.

At last, I heard the beep-beep of the car doors unlocking. Then the interior lights came on. Bob started the engine, switched on the headlights, and returned to help me to the car.

Getting in, I noticed that the neon beer signs that had served as a beacon to us less than an hour before now hung darkened in windows. Dark, silent windows beyond which, mere seconds earlier, a room full of barflies stood watching us run out as the music on the jukebox blared. We had enjoyed beers and studied a mural in a place that now seemingly had been empty all along.

As the car swung around, throwing gravel behind us, we noticed that no cars remained in the parking lot. Not a soul had left, but not a single vehicle remained. The tires screeched as we turned onto the main highway driving in stunned silence away from The Roadhouse Saloon as quickly as the car would take us.

Neither of us knew what to say. Neither of us knew what had

happened. We both just stared out ahead at the road in front of us. After several tense minutes, Bob turned to me. "Did that really just happen?" he asked.

"I think so," I replied.

"What the Hell *was* that?"

"I have no idea, but I'm sure glad we left when we did," I said.

I did not want to think what might have happened had we not taken a special interest in the mural, had we not noticed the people in it, or the figures appearing in the swinging doors. I glanced down at my cane, grateful that one small detail, a woman with a cane, made it possible for us to escape in quite possibly the nick of time from that highly improbable situation.

"That really happened. Whoa." Bob shook his head.

The next day Bob and I asked each other to confirm details of our early morning experience at The Roadhouse Saloon. I told my sisters and cousins the story. One or two thought I made it all up, but most of my sisters and others who knew me best believed my unlikely tale. They wanted to see The Roadhouse Saloon for themselves. I had no intention of returning in the dark, so we made plans to go there one afternoon in the week following.

As we drove to The Roadhouse Saloon in broad daylight, my companions listened with bated breath while I repeated my story, explaining every detail I could recall. Everyone's excitement—and my trepidation—grew as we turned onto the county road leading to the parking lot. It looked quite different in the daylight. We could see light in the windows behind the neon beer signs. We parked near the door beside a few other cars in the parking lot.

Walking through the door, I noticed the very same horseshoe-shaped bar. I looked to my right hoping in vain to see the ladies who sat there the last time. Searching for the bartender, I found only a young woman serving drinks from behind the bar. I saw the bathroom exactly where I had used it in the wee hours of the morning. Nothing had changed in the bathroom when I went with my sister-in-law to check it out except for the half-full trash can.

The pool table stood unused near the restrooms. The dance floor, however, looked completely different. Instead of a vast open space, several tables and chairs filled most of it. I searched for the Wurlitzer that played only one song all night, only to find a modern digital machine filled with CDs. I had taken a particular interest in the vintage jukebox that had stood in its place less than a week prior. The replacement of a large, heavy machine which I had studied closely disturbed me greatly. Despite my certainty that this machine hadn't been there, I searched the song list for Chubby Checker with no luck. I tried to explain to my companions how odd it all seemed. It felt completely different. I could not have mistaken the song that played exclusively and repeatedly the night Bob and I had stopped there. Then I scanned the place to no avail, hoping to find at least one familiar face from that strange and terrifying night. Finally, I approached the young woman tending bar.

Ordering drinks for our party, I nonchalantly asked, "So where's the other bartender?"

"What other bartender?" she replied, popping caps off bottles.

"That young guy with short dark hair and big muscles."

"There's no guy like that here. I'm the only bartender except for my dad, and that doesn't sound like him."

"No," I went on. "I saw him here last Saturday when we stopped late—somewhere between two and three in the morning."

"Not here," she said. "No possible way! My dad owns this place. Just me and him work the bar, and I closed at eleven last weekend."

I turned to see the shocked expression and terrified eyes on my sister-in-law's face as she stood next to me. I thanked the bartender and passed out bottles to my cohorts.

"This is all just too weird," I said to them, "Let's check out the mural."

Together we passed the tables and chairs that filled most of the dance floor and walked up to the painting. I pointed out all of the figures and described their role in the previous week's strange events. I told them again how the piano player had dropped coin after coin into the Wurlitzer, playing the same song over and over again. My sister found it both interesting and disturbing that the guy playing music in the mural also played the soundtrack to my crazy and unlikely experience. Everything in the painting looked exactly as I remembered it, save for one detail. No figures appeared in the swinging doors of the saloon. The entryway into that mural stood vacant and inviting, perhaps waiting for other late-night travelers to enter The Roadhouse Saloon.

EPILOGUE

Good spirit of the sacred place,
Grant me blessing, grant me grace.
Keep me safe in night and day,
And hold me ever in your sway.
Spirit of Water, Earth, and Green,
Grant me sight for things unseen.

I HEARD THESE WORDS RESONATE IN THE DEPTHS OF MY SOUL one Winter Solstice day as I walked alone along the banks of the river where two streams unite. It is a magical place where multiple springs offer the sweetest, purest water bubbling up from deep beneath the earth's surface, into the light. The invigorating water is a gift to all living things. Light snow covered fallen leaves in this stead where the veil remains ever-thin between the corporeal world and what lies beyond, a place where I find a visceral connection to all things sacred.

I went there seeking solace and comfort for the difficulties in my life. Troubles with children and struggles in my relationship with David drove me there, for I knew not what. I just knew that I needed to go there alone. I left a gathering at home and headed to the spring.

There I felt a deep connection to my ancestors, angels, and guides. I heard the voice of all things holy, who gifted me my mantra, which I use daily as I light candles on my altar for meditation.

The events in my life, and my willingness to see beyond the obvious, have served to keep me on a path that leads me, continuously, toward the gate between here and everywhere. This awareness, that so much more lies just beyond our physical sight, has made for an unusual life, a life between realities, a liminal life. From the spirits of my childhood home to many other encounters beyond the corporeal. On this path, I have grown as a gatekeeper or spirit medium. My task now is to apply this unusual knowledge, or gift, as some have called it. I continue unflinchingly to seek the good in all things and use my abilities to bring comfort or help to those who suffer, whether living, ghost, spirit, or never-living being.

I am one of many who tend the gate, both here and among the many other realities that trickle through from time to time revealing so many possibilities, such wonders. We are not alone. *We are never alone.* We are all, every one of us, moving endlessly toward the gate. It is the choice of each of us to recognize it, or to live in denial that one day all things will become one with this amazing and wonder-filled universe.

If you have enjoyed this book, point your browser to:

www.parkhurstbrothers.com